Incorruptible Bodies and Bilocation Miracles Across World Religions

William Bodri

Copyright © 2024 William Bodri. All rights reserved. No part of this book may be used or reproduced in any manner whatsoever without the written permission of the publisher, except in cases of brief quotations in articles and reviews. The content of this book is for informational purposes only and is not intended to diagnose, treat, cure, or prevent any disease or health condition. You understand that this book is not intended as a substitute for consultation with a licensed health practitioner. Please consult with your own physician or healthcare specialist regarding the information made available in this book. The use of this book implies your acceptance of this disclaimer.

First Edition – June 2025

Top Shape Publishing LLC
1135 Terminal Way Suite 209
Reno, NV 89502

ISBN: 978-1-7370320-7-6

DEDICATION

To ardent religious practitioners who have travelled to personally witness the incorruptible bodies of saints, who have personally seen cases of bilocation or simply heard of either of these phenomena, and desire the explanation offered in world religions. Sometimes the explanations may seem repetitive, but revisiting the same concepts are to make sure that you understand concepts that are foreign to most people due to the lack of prior exposure.

CONTENTS

	Acknowledgments	i
1	Stories of Bilocation Across Religions	1
2	Our Five Spiritual Bodies	40
3	Proven Cases of Incorruptible Bodies	87
4	The Yin-Yang Emotional Upheaval of Kundalini Purification	119
5	12+ Years of Internal Energy Cleansing	144
6	The Non-Sectarian Ladder of Spiritual Progress	166

ACKNOWLEDGMENTS

On this topic, we all owe a debt of thanks to *The Incorruptibles*, by Joan Carroll Cruz, which deals with the uncorrupted bodies of various Catholic saints. I have personally seen quite several uncorrupted bodies of enlightened monks in China and Thailand, and also seen demonstrations of the psychic powers of various eastern masters. We owe a debt to the many people who have preserved these bodies and the miraculous stories of saints, with reverence and devotion, because they have enabled us to recognize a commonality in the results of the spiritual path.

CHAPTER 1:
STORIES OF BILOCATION ACROSS RELIGIONS

Bilocation, or sometimes multilocation, is the reported ability to appear in two (or more) different locations simultaneously. Bilocation is considered impossible according to the known laws of nature, but throughout the centuries this miracle has been attributed to various spiritual figures in many spiritual traditions, and reported by trustworthy witnesses who verified the accounts. This includes figures from Christianity, Hinduism, Buddhism, Islam, Judaism and other spiritual traditions.

CHRISTIANITY

The most famous modern cases of bilocation primarily involve Catholic saints and religious figures from the 20th century. However, a variety of cases can be found throughout Catholic history.

For instance, **St. Anthony of Padua** (1195-1231) is often associated with bilocation in the Catholic tradition. He reportedly appeared in Lisbon to save his father from false accusations while simultaneously preaching in Padua. Franciscan records also claim he preached in two churches at the same time.

The "flying saint," **St. Joseph of Cupertino** (1603–1663), was also said to be capable of bilocation. While praying in his cell, he was also seen helping construction workers lift heavy stones at a distant church. Because of his many miracles his case will be discussed later in more detail.

Christian mysticism openly recognizes bilocation as a real occurrence. In fact, in Catholic theology it is seen as a divine gift, bestowed upon those of exceptional spiritual advancement, for the benefit of others. It is considered a way for a saint to be present in a location where they are not physically located in order to aid those in need, or to fulfill a particular task.

Several saints other than Saint Anthony of Padua – such as St. Padre Pio, St. Faustina, St. Martin de Porres, and St. Francis Xavier, and St. Alphonsus Liguori – are known for witnessed, confirmed reports of bilocation, meaning that witnesses could vouch for them appearing in two places at the same time. To explain this topic, let us first review the cases of a few famous Christian saints known to have demonstrated bilocation. The beloved Saint Padre Pio is perhaps the most well-documented modern example, so we will start with his story.

Padre Pio (1887-1968), an Italian Capuchin friar canonized in 2002, became renowned for numerous supernatural gifts that became known all over modern Italy, and then the world. In fact, his case sparked a renewed interest in the Catholic Church and was one of the reasons that Italy was able to resist Communism.

As to bilocation, the accounts of Padre Pio's abilities to appear in two places at the same time are numerous. In a notable instance, Padre Pio reportedly appeared in the Vatican while physically remaining at his monastery in San Giovanni Rotondo. Don Orione, a holy priest, reported seeing Padre Pio praying in the crypt at the tomb of Pius X, convincing skeptics like Pope Benedict XV and Cardinal Merry del Val of his authenticity. This bilocation was notable because hearing confessions requires physical presence for sacramental validity. A bishop visiting the Pope claimed to have seen Padre Pio there, only to learn the friar had never left his monastery hundreds of miles away.

During WWII, Allied bombers were tasked with attacking San Giovanni Rotondo, where Padre Pio lived. Padre Pio demonstrated dramatic bilocation when he appeared in the air over San Giovanni Rotondo, preventing American bombers from releasing their payload and fulfilling his promise to protect the town while his physical body remained in the monastery. Pilots from multiple squadrons reported seeing a bearded priest in the sky, frantically waving to stop them. The figure matched Padre Pio's description, and no bombs were ever dropped on the village. When shown Padre Pio's photograph later, American and British crew members always identified him as the mysterious figure who had appeared in the air.

Perhaps most remarkably, numerous devotees reported Padre Pio appearing at their bedsides during serious illnesses or moments of crisis – sometimes in places as far away as the United States – while witnesses at San Giovanni Rotondo confirmed his simultaneous physical presence at the monastery. A woman in Italy, gravely ill, reported that Padre Pio appeared at her bedside, blessed her, and promised her recovery. She kissed his stigmatized hands, and he vanished. Afterwards she recovered within days. Meanwhile, witnesses in San Giovanni Rotondo confirmed Padre Pio had not left the friary, and he later described the event as an "extension of his personality," which we will later see refers to having attained the ability generate additional spiritual bodies.

When he was alive Padre Pio was seen in various locations worldwide, including the Holy Land and the United States, despite rarely leaving his parish in San Giovanni Rotondo.

Sister Rita Montello (1920-1992), an Augustinian sister connected to Padre Pio who also received the stigmata, had many extraordinary gifts such as visibly seeing her guardian angel, the gift of prophecy, reading of hearts, and bilocation. During the last years of her life, she nourished herself exclusively on the Eucharist rather than food, which is another miracle often reported of Christian saints.

Padre Pio treated her as a spiritual daughter, often calling her his "bambino" because of her innocence. She reported to others that she often went in bilocation on missions all over the globe with Padre Pio, such as going together to Budapest to comfort Cardinal Mindszenty in jail, to visit other victims of the Soviet government, or even to help soldiers in danger or in concentration camps.

Sister Rita said that she went together with Padre Pio many times to help soldiers in danger and to take humanitarian aid. One time, she said, "We went to a concentration camp in Germany to free an Italian soldier. The guards thought we were spies and shot at us, but the shots did not do anything to us." Sister Cherubina Fascia (a fellow nun and contemporary of Sister Rita) confirmed these accounts, stating that Sister Rita spoke of these events with absolute conviction, and Father Franco D'Anastasio (a priest who collected much of the information about the life of Sister Rita) documented her claims.

The book, *La "Bambina" di padre Pio: Rita Montella* (Citta Ideale, 2003), by Christina Siccardia and translated by Angelica Avcikurt, reported that her bilocation body could disappear in front of you, which is a tale told by many who have witnessed this miracle for other saints, gurus or sages:

> *Sister Cherubina Fascia, who was a spiritual daughter of Padre Pio, a devoted friend to Sister Rita and a disciple of Father Teofilo Dal Pozzo who was later the spiritual director of Sister Rita, was told the following by the Abbess of the convent of Sister Rita, Abbess Matilda:* "One day Sister Rita came to my room and told me that Padre Pio had asked her to accompany him to visit Cardinal Mindszenty in jail to take him what he needs to celebrate Mass. I answered that perhaps she wanted my permission!? I also asked her when she had to go and she quickly answered: Tomorrow night. I in turn said to her: Take everything you need and bring it to my room beforehand. When the time comes for you to leave, you will come to my room for the things and then you can go. She did as she was told. In my room, which I had locked, I waited while praying; my heart was beating very fast. At a certain point I heard a knock and I said: Come in. Despite the fact that the door was locked, she entered, took everything she needed from the table and started to leave. While she was leaving, I tried to follow her, since the door to my room was now open. At a certain moment she disappeared in front of my very eyes. Then I went quickly to her room to check if her body was there, and she was lying in bed. Then I returned to my room to find the door locked. I had to use my key to enter and I locked it once more. I continued to pray waiting for Sister Rita to return. After a while she came back in exactly the same way; she knocked, entered through the locked door, returned everything to the table and said goodnight."[1]

Sister Rita had the gift of prophecy and knew that her spiritual director Father Teofilo was going to fall into a 12-meter deep ditch. The priest was walking down the street after visiting a convent, and Sister Rita appeared in bilocation at the moment the priest fell into the ditch injuring his head and

---

[1] Accessed May 5, 2025: https://luisapiccarreta.com/other-category/cristina-montella-sister-rita-of-the-holy-spirit-the-little-girl-of-padre-pio/

his back. He did not die because Sister Rita rescued him. His glasses and the eggs he was carrying did not even get broken. Injured, he was sure he was accompanied home by Sister Rita who was invisible. He felt someone was holding him and he also could smell the mystical perfume she emanated.

The Mother Superior later asked Sister Rita if it was true that she had helped him and she replied, "See for yourself, my habit is all full of mud." She also asked God to let her take some of the priest's suffering after the fall. She obtained her request and suffered for a while until the suffering suddenly disappeared.

The next case is that of **Saint Alphonsus Liguori** (1696-1787), the founder of the Redemptorists and a Doctor of the Church, who was witnessed in deep prayer at his monastery in Pagani, Italy while simultaneously was seen kneeling at the bedside of Pope Clement XIII in Rome as the pope lay dying. Multiple witnesses, including fellow priests and laypeople, also reported seeing Alphonsus hearing confessions in two different churches at the same time. In another instance, a man on his deathbed in Spain claimed that Alphonsus visited him, heard his confession, and comforted him. Later investigations confirmed that Alphonsus had been in Italy at the time.

St. Francis Xavier (1506-1552), a Spanish Jesuit missionary, is another exemplar of bilocation. His frequent bilocations were well-documented by eyewitnesses, often occurring during his preaching missions. In the East Indies, Francis was reported to have preached simultaneously in different villages, sometimes miles apart. Witnesses, including native converts, described seeing him deliver sermons in their locales at the same time, with each group believing he was physically present. His biographer noted these bilocations as "quite ordinary" due to their frequency.

During a storm in the Malacca Strait, Francis was also seen aboard a ship, calming the crew and guiding it to safety, while simultaneously documented as being in a distant mission in India. Sailors later testified to his presence, describing his calm demeanor amidst the chaos.

St. Joseph of Cupertino (1603–1663), an Italian Conventual Franciscan friar and mystic, is renowned for many miraculous phenomena.

While his levitations are more widely documented, accounts of his bilocation are also recorded in historical sources, particularly in hagiographies, canonization testimonies, and Catholic devotional literature, such as those found in secondary works like *The Franciscan Book of Saints* or *They Flew: A History of the Impossible* by Carlos Eire and *Mysteries, Marvels, Miracles*.

One notable story involves an elderly gentleman from Cupertino named Octavius Piccinno, affectionately called "Father." Piccinno asked St. Joseph to assist him at the hour of his death. Joseph promised to do so, adding, "I shall assist you, even though I should be in Rome." At the time of Piccinno's final illness, Joseph was indeed in Rome, far from Cupertino. As Piccinno neared death, witnesses, including Sr. Teresa Fatali of the Third Order, reported seeing St. Joseph at Piccinno's bedside, speaking with him. Sr. Teresa, astonished, asked, "Fr. Joseph, how did you come?" He replied, "I came to assist the soul of 'Father,'" and then vanished. This account suggests Joseph bilocated from Rome to Cupertino to fulfill his promise.

The thirteen volumes of St. Joseph's canonization process, preserved in the Vatican Archives, include testimonies from numerous witnesses – princes, cardinals, bishops, and doctors – who claimed to have observed or heard of his bilocation. While specific details of every instance are not fully accessible in English, these records note that Joseph was commonly seen in different locations simultaneously, often during moments of spiritual significance, such as aiding the sick or dying. For example, he was reported to appear in places where his intercession was sought, even when he was known to be elsewhere, such as in a friary or during prayer. These accounts were considered credible by contemporaries and contributed to his canonization in 1767.

St. Martin de Porres (1579-1639), a Peruvian Dominican lay brother of mixed race, was known for his humility, healing, and mystical gifts, often to aid the poor and sick. He was known for bilocating to various locations, including China, Japan and northern Africa while residing in Lima. His incorruptible body, exhumed in 1664, emitted a floral scent when exhumed and those relics are now venerated in Lima, Peru.

As an example of bilocation, a merchant in Mexico, facing ruin, reported that Martin once appeared to him, offering guidance and supplies to save his business. Upon returning to Lima, the merchant learned Martin had never left Peru. The priests at Martin's monastery confirmed he remained there, yet Martin later acknowledged assisting the man supernaturally.

St. Gerard Majella (1726-1755), an Italian Redemptorist lay brother, is celebrated for his deep piety, miracles, and mystical gifts, including bilocation on multiple occasions. Known as the patron saint of expectant mothers, Gerard's bilocation accounts often involved acts of charity, spiritual aid, or protection. Below are three well-documented stories illustrating his bilocation, drawn from historical records and testimonies collected during his canonization process.

During a harsh winter, Gerard was known for aiding the poor around Materdomini, where he served. A poor family, stranded without food or firewood miles away, reported that a young man in a Redemptorist habit appeared at their door with a bundle of supplies, including bread and wood. He blessed their home and vanished. When the family later recounted the story in town, they identified Gerard as the visitor based on descriptions of his appearance. However, Redemptorist records and testimonies from his community confirmed that Gerard had been engaged in manual labor at the monastery during the exact time of the visit, with no opportunity to travel. When questioned, Gerard smiled and said, "God provides for those in need," neither confirming nor denying the bilocation.

While stationed at the Redemptorist house in Caposele, Italy, Gerard was reported to have bilocated to assist a dying man in a distant town. A family in a neighboring region, unknown to the Redemptorists, was praying for spiritual assistance as their patriarch faced death in despair, unable to reconcile with God. Witnesses testified that a young religious brother, matching Gerard's description, appeared at the man's bedside, prayed with him, and administered spiritual comfort, leading to a peaceful death. The family later visited Caposele to thank the Redemptorists, only to learn that Gerard had not left the monastery during the time of the incident. His superiors and fellow brothers confirmed his physical presence in Caposele, and Gerard humbly attributed the event to God's will, saying he had been "sent" to help the man.

These stories were recorded by contemporaries, including Redemptorist priests and laypeople, and scrutinized during Gerard's canonization process in 1904. Bilocation was one of many miracles attributed to him, often linked to his intense prayer life and devotion to God's will. The Catholic Church's investigation into Gerard's life included testimonies from multiple witnesses, such as families and clergy, who corroborated the timing and details of these events. His bilocations were seen as extensions of his mission to serve the poor and suffering.

Venerable Archbishop Teofilo Camomot (1914-1988), a native of Carcar, Cebu, Philippines, was a Roman Catholic prelate celebrated for his heroic virtues, Franciscan-like poverty, and spiritual gifts, including multiple cases of bilocation. Known for his dedication to the poor and pastoral zeal, Camomot's bilocation accounts often involved aiding the sick or dying. These stories are drawn from testimonies collected during his cause for beatification, as well as accounts from contemporaries like Cardinal Ricardo Vidal, and are part of the historical record supporting his path to sainthood.

Zenaida Paninsoro, a member of the Legion of Mary in Carcar, shared a striking account of Camomot's bilocation. On a particular morning at 10 a.m., she attended a wedding in Carcar officiated by Camomot, fondly called "Nyor Lolong." The following day, she was surprised to receive gifts from two women who claimed they had been with Camomot at the same time – 10 a.m. the previous day – praying for the healing of their mother in a different location. The women described Camomot's presence and prayers in detail, and their mother recovered shortly after. Paninsoro confirmed Camomot had been physically present at the wedding, as she and other parishioners witnessed him performing the ceremony. This simultaneous appearance in two places, supported by multiple witnesses, was reported as a clear instance of bilocation.

Another account involves Camomot's bilocation to aid a sick parishioner while he was known to be at the Daughters of Saint Teresa (DST) convent in Valladolid, Carcar. A family in a nearby village reported that Camomot visited their home to pray over a gravely ill relative, offering comfort and blessings that led to the person's recovery. The family noted the exact time of his visit and described his calm demeanor and distinctive vestments. Meanwhile, sisters at the DST convent, which Camomot founded, confirmed he was physically present with them, engaged in spiritual direction or prayer, at the same time. When later approached about the incident, Camomot humbly deflected questions, attributing any miracles to God's grace. This story, circulated among devotees, was included in the testimonies submitted for his beatification process.

The late Cardinal Ricardo Vidal also authenticated his presence at a meeting while he was simultaneously reported to be in a mountain village administering last rites.

These bilocation stories are part of the evidence supporting Camomot's cause for sainthood, which began in 2010 under Cardinal Vidal. On May 21, 2022, Pope Francis declared Camomot "Venerable" for his heroic virtues, and his cause continues to progress.

The accounts were rigorously examined by the Archdiocese of Cebu, with 45 witnesses interviewed for the "Positio" submitted to the Vatican in 2020. Testimonies from clergy, like Vidal, and laypeople, like Paninsoro, provide credibility. Camomot's incorrupt body, exhumed in 2009, further bolstered his reputation for holiness.

Another famous case of bilocation is that of **Saint Thérèse of Lisieux**. In the blood-soaked trenches of World War I, many French soldiers reported extraordinary encounters with a young Carmelite nun who had died nearly two decades before the conflict began. Saint Thérèse of Lisieux, known as "The Little Flower," officially passed away in 1897 from tuberculosis at the age of 24, yet numerous accounts suggest her spiritual presence brought comfort to soldiers facing the horrors of modern trench warfare. Before her death, Thérèse promised: "After my death, I will let fall a shower of roses. I will spend my heaven doing good upon earth." For many French soldiers, this promise manifested in remarkable ways during the war.

Countless testimonies emerged from the front lines describing a young nun appearing to wounded or dying men, offering comfort and sometimes even healing. Soldiers who had carried her image or writings reported protection in seemingly impossible circumstances. Some described a distinct scent of roses amid the stench of battle – a sign traditionally associated with Saint Thérèse. The scent of violets, on the other hand, is traditionally associated with Padre Pio. Mystical fragrances (often called "the odor of sanctity") are typically reported in connection with various saints or their worldly remains.

One French officer wrote in his journal about a mysterious nun who appeared to him after he was wounded in no-man's land, helping him remain conscious until stretcher-bearers arrived. When later shown various images of nuns, he immediately identified Thérèse, though he had never seen her likeness before.

Another widely circulated account involved a group of soldiers trapped in a collapsed bunker after heavy shelling. They collectively reported seeing a Carmelite nun showing them a way out through the rubble – a passage their rescuers later confirmed should not have existed given the structure's damage.

The frequency of these reported appearances earned Thérèse the unofficial title 'Saint of the Trenches' among French soldiers. Many carried her picture or medals alongside their military identification. Letters home frequently mentioned her protection or intervention, contributing to her growing reputation for spiritual bilocation.

The phenomenon wasn't limited to Catholic soldiers – men of various faiths and even non-believers reported encounters with the young nun, often only learning her identity later when describing their experiences to chaplains or fellow soldiers.

While Thérèse was not officially canonized until 1925, these wartime accounts contributed significantly to her cause for sainthood. The Church never officially declared these as instances of bilocation but acknowledged them as examples of her extraordinary spiritual intercession.

EASTERN ORTHODOX CHURCH

Bilocation is also a well-documented occurrence in Orthodox Christian spirituality, too. In the Orthodox branch of Christianity, bilocation is understood as a grace (χάρις) granted by God for specific purposes, often tied to prayer, spiritual warfare, or divine intervention. Some of those monks who demonstrated bilocation include the following:

St. Seraphim of Sarov (18th–19th Century), one of Russia's most revered saints, was a monk, mystic, and starets (spiritual elder) known for his asceticism, prophecy, and miracles. He is a patron saint of Russia and a central figure in Russian Orthodoxy who is also known for his powers of bilocation. One story goes that a noblewoman visiting St. Seraphim's hermitage found him praying in his cell, yet that same evening, he appeared to her sick daughter in another city, healing her. When the woman returned to thank him, he smiled and said, "What are you thanking me for? It was God's mercy."

A monk at the Sarov Monastery, struggling with despair, reported that St. Seraphim appeared in his cell, offering spiritual counsel and comfort. At the time, St. Seraphim was known to be in reclusion in his forest hermitage, miles away, suggesting bilocation. A villager near Sarov also claimed that during a near-drowning incident, St. Seraphim appeared on the riverbank, guiding him to safety. Witnesses later confirmed that St. Seraphim was at the monastery, engaged in prayer, at the time of the incident.

A saint venerated in the Greek Orthodox Church, **St. Gerasimos of Kefalonia** (1506–1579), is the patron saint of Kefalonia, known for his ascetic life and miracles, including healings and exorcisms. His relics remain incorrupt at the Monastery of St. Gerasimos in Kefalonia.

While St. Gerasimos is primarily known for miracles involving his relics and intercessions, some local traditions and hagiographies suggest he appeared in multiple places to aid those in need, a phenomenon akin to bilocation. As an example, according to local tradition in Kefalonia, St. Gerasimos was seen by sailors during a storm at sea, calming the waters and guiding their ship to safety. At the same time, he was known to be praying in his monastery on the island. The sailors later visited the monastery to thank him, only to learn he had not physically left, suggesting bilocation.

A modern Greek saint, **St. Nektarios of Aegina** (1846–1920), is one of the most beloved figures in the Greek Orthodox Church, known for his humility, theological writings, and numerous miracles. He was a bishop and founder of a monastery on Aegina. A devotee recounted that while St. Nektarios was at his monastery on Aegina, he appeared to a gravely ill woman in a remote village, praying over her and leading to her recovery. When the woman's family visited Aegina to thank him, they learned he had not left the island during that time, implying bilocation.

A pilgrim lost in the hills near Aegina claimed that St. Nektarios appeared to guide him to safety. Monks at the monastery confirmed that the saint had been in prayer at the time, suggesting he was miraculously present elsewhere. These accounts are drawn from biographies and miracle collections, such as those in the *Lives of the Saints Calendar* and oral traditions among Greek Orthodox faithful.

St. John of Kronstadt (1829–1908), a Russian Orthodox priest and wonderworker, was known for his fervent prayers, charitable works, and miracles. He is the patron saint of St. Petersburg and a prominent figure in Russian Orthodoxy. St. John's intense prayer life and miraculous interventions led to reports of his presence in multiple locations, particularly when answering urgent calls for help. His bilocation is noted in accounts of his intercessory miracles.

As examples, a family in Moscow, praying for their dying child, reported that St. John appeared at their home, prayed over the child, and the child recovered. At the same time, St. John was documented as serving Liturgy in Kronstadt, hundreds of miles away.

Sailors caught in a storm off the Gulf of Finland reported seeing St. John on their ship, calming the crew and guiding them to safety. Parish records showed he was conducting services in Kronstadt at the time.

A prisoner facing execution claimed that St. John appeared in his cell, offering prayers and reassurance. The prisoner's sentence was miraculously commuted, and it was later confirmed that St. John was in Kronstadt during the visitation.

These accounts are recorded in biographies of St. John, such as those in *Lives of the Saints* by the Orthodox Church in America and Russian Orthodox hagiographies.

St. Spyridon of Trimythous (4th Century) was participating in the First Ecumenical Council of Nicaea (325 AD), where bishops gathered to debate the Arian heresy. One night, fellow bishops noticed he had left the assembly without explanation. The next day, a local farmer arrived at the council, distraught and claiming that his oxen had become stuck in deep mud during a storm and were at risk of drowning. Suddenly, a mysterious bishop (Spyridon) appeared, prayed, and miraculously freed the animals. The farmer recognized Spyridon from church and came to thank him. The bishops were shocked because Spyridon had been with them the entire night in council. When questioned, Spyridon remained silent, but his absence at the exact time of the miracle suggested bilocation.

In his book *Athonite Fathers and Athonite Matters*, **St. Paisios the Athonite** (1924–1994) relayed a story of an elder who, while praying in his cell, was seen guiding lost hikers on a mountain trail. When the hikers later found the elder they believed had saved them – praying in his cell – he denied having left his hermitage that day. He told them, "Perhaps an angel took my form."

St. Paisios himself is a famous for the powers of clairvoyance, healing, and for having wild animals follow his commands. Multiple monks and pilgrims have testified that St. Paisios was seen in two places at once, most notably attending Divine Liturgy at his own hermitage while simultaneously appearing at a distant monastery's service. Some claimed he also materialized to comfort distressed visitors while never physically leaving his cell.

HINDUISM

Like Christianity, Hinduism has centuries of stories where "enlightened" spiritual masters and yogis were witnessed appearing in two or more places at once, which is classic bilocation. In some cases, a spiritual master was seen in multiple locations at the same time.

In the yogic tradition, the *Yoga Vasistha* and *Shiva Sutras* describe bilocation (*dūra-sravana*) as a sign of advanced consciousness that is attained through meditative efforts and other spiritual cultivation practices. In other words, it is attained if the individual devotes themselves to spiritual exercises and makes tremendous progress along this path.

Focusing on just our modern era, several bilocation stories involving Hindu saints include the following:

Neem Karoli Baba (1900-1973), a revered Hindu saint, is often said to have appeared in multiple locations simultaneously. *The Miracle of Love*, by Ram Dass (1979), reports a story where a devotee named Dada Mukerjee reported that Maharaj-ji was physically present at his ashram in Kainchi (Uttarakhand) when another disciple, who was waiting at a distant train station, suddenly saw him there. The guru gave him specific instructions, then vanished. Later, the disciple returned to Kainchi and found Maharaj-ji sitting exactly as he'd been before – never having "left."

In the 1970s, an American devotee claimed to see Maharaj-ji in California, where he materialized to offer comfort. Simultaneously, others swore he was in Vrindavan (India) giving darshan. When asked, Maharaj-ji laughed and said, "I sit in one place, but my *lila* (divine play) is everywhere."

A shopkeeper in Delhi insisted Maharaj-ji had visited his stall for tea one morning, describing his orange robe and wooden sandals. That same morning, devotees in Vrindavan (200 km away) were with him in a temple. When confronted, Maharaj-ji merely smiled and said, "Can't a man enjoy two cups of tea?"

These are just three of the multiple stories of bilocation concerning this saint.

Bhagawan Nityananda of Ganeshpuri (1897–1961), also known simply as Swami Nityananda, was an Indian guru revered for his spiritual presence and miraculous abilities, including multiple cases of bilocation.

For instance, at one time a group of devotees in Kerala claimed they saw Nityananda accepting food at a temple feast, while villagers in Tamil Nadu (over 300 km away) simultaneously reported him blessing them in their fields. When questioned, he reportedly laughed and said, "Does the wind not blow in many places at once?"

Nityananda: The Divine Presence (K.R. Paramahamsa) records the story of a sick child in Mangalore who was said to have been touched and healed by Nityananda, while on the same day, a farmer in Coothampally (Karnataka) swore the saint appeared to him in his field. Later, when devotees compared notes, Nityananda dismissed it, saying, "God's work happens in many ways."

A merchant traveling by train from Bombay to Varanasi claimed to see Nityananda meditating under a tree near Nasik. Upon arriving in Varanasi, he was shocked to find the saint already there, waiting for him at the Kashi Vishwanath Temple.

Lahiri Mahasaya (1828–1895), the renowned Kriya Yoga master and guru of Paramahansa Yogananda, was widely reported to have exhibited the siddhi (power) of bilocation. The reports come from his disciples, though specific details are often scarce, and are also documented in spiritual texts like Paramahansa Yogananda's *Autobiography of a Yogi*. According to followers, he could appear in multiple locations simultaneously, such as being in his Varanasi home while also manifesting elsewhere to guide or assist devotees. Here are a few key stories:

Autobiography of a Yogi (Chapter 31), by Paramahansa Yogananda, reports that a disciple in Varanasi was speaking with Lahiri Mahasaya at his home when another devotee arrived, claiming he had just seen the master in Allahabad (over 200 km away) giving spiritual instructions. Lahiri Mahasaya simply smiled and said, "The body is a mere shadow of the soul. The soul can be wherever it wishes."

At another time, Lahiri Mahasaya was summoned to testify in a court case in Varanasi. While he was physically present in the courtroom, a respected judge in Calcutta swore under oath that the yogi had appeared before him at the same time to discuss a legal matter. The court records reportedly noted this inexplicable event.

A skeptical merchant in Lucknow once mocked Lahiri Mahasaya's reputed powers, saying, "If he's so great, let him come here!" That evening, the yogi appeared before him in the tea shop, silently sipping tea before vanishing. The stunned merchant later traveled to Varanasi to apologize.

Sri Yukteswar Giri (1855–1936), the revered guru of Paramahansa Yogananda and a realized master of Kriya Yoga, was known for his profound wisdom and occasional displays of miraculous powers, including bilocation. Though he rarely demonstrated such abilities openly (emphasizing inner realization over miracles), a few well-documented accounts from disciples and texts like *Autobiography of a Yogi* attest to these special abilities. Here are the most notable stories.

A lawyer in Calcutta once needed Sri Yukteswar's testimony for a case but assumed the guru would refuse to travel. To his shock, Sri Yukteswar appeared in the courtroom, gave his statement, and vanished. Later, the lawyer visited the ashram to thank him – only to find Sri Yukteswar sitting calmly, claiming he had never left.

One of the most profound accounts of Sri Yukteswar's bilocation occurs after his physical death, as recorded in Paramahansa Yogananda's *Autobiography of a Yogi* (Chapter 43: "The Resurrection of Sri Yukteswar"). After Sri Yukteswar's physical passing in Puri (March 1936), Yogananda was grieving deeply. Months later, while staying at a disciple's home in Mumbai (formerly Bombay), Yogananda felt an overwhelming urge to visit the seaside. As Yogananda stood on the beach, Sri Yukteswar suddenly appeared beside him in radiant, flesh-and-blood form, wearing a saffron robe and the same sandals he'd worn in life. Yogananda, overcome with joy, touched his guru's body and found it solid and warm – not a ghostly apparition. Their conversation, reported in *Autobiography of a Yoga* (1946), ran as follows:

"Master!" I cried, falling to my knees. "Is it you? Is it truly you?"

"Yes, my son, it is I." Sri Yukteswar's voice was resonant, his smile celestial. "I have risen in a body exactly like my earthly one – though it is now imperishable and composed of etherealized atoms. This is no ghost you see, but your guru in flesh and bone!"

I clasped his feet in reverence; they were solid, warm with life. "How is this possible, Gurudeva?"

"A master who has merged with the Cosmic Consciousness can reappear in any form at will," he replied. "This body is a materialized thought-projection, as real as your own."

Sri Yukteswar explained that he now resided in the "subtle astral world" but had temporarily reassembled his atomic structure to visit Yogananda. He revealed: "Though I have resurrected this body, it is not exactly the same as before. I have given it a certain ethereal quality, like the body of a siddha (perfected being). A saint who has achieved final union with Spirit can reappear on earth in any number of simultaneously visible forms. These are not mere reflections like the images of a cinema, but are individualized manifestations of the master's divine life force."

For over three hours, they walked and talked. Sri Yukteswar taught Yogananda about the afterlife realms (astral and causal worlds, how advanced yogis can manifest physical forms, and the immortality of the soul. In these talks, Yukteswar emphasized that the so-called "dead" are fully alive in another dimension, and that death is but a change of address.

Devraha Baba (?-1990) was a revered Indian Siddha Yogi saint, often referred to as the "Ageless Yogi" due to the mystery surrounding his age. His miracles were documented by Sri Ramana Maharshi's disciples, who acknowledged Baba's powers, as well as by Paramahansa Yogananda's lineage, which compared him to Lahiri Mahasaya.

A mystic yogi known for miraculous feats, Devraha Baba reportedly bilocated during an incident where he was seen addressing a gathering in Lucknow while simultaneously traveling by car from Delhi to the same location.

An account from Swami Satyamitranand Giri's Memoirs said that in the 1970s, a group of devotees in Vrindavan received darshan (blessings) from Devraha Baba as he sat on his elevated wooden platform (machan). That same evening, pilgrims in Ayodhya (over 600 km away) reported seeing him giving spiritual advice near the Sarayu River. When questioned, Baba simply smiled and said: "The body is a toy of the soul. The soul can play in many places at once."

His bilocation abilities were also witnessed by Indian politicians. In 1982, during a political crisis, Prime Minister Indira Gandhi sent officials to consult Devraha Baba in Varanasi (Kashi). While they spoke to him there, a cabinet minister in Delhi swore he saw Baba meditating near India Gate. Later, the officials returned to Delhi and confirmed Baba had never left Kashi. He responded cryptically: "When the country calls, how can I not be present?"

Once **Bhagavan Ramana Maharshi** (1879-1950) was caught by his childhood friend Ranjan (Velacheri Ranga Iyer) emanating a body double (*yang-shen nirmanakaya*) whilst asleep, which is another way of describing bilocation using the technical terms of Buddhism and Taoism. Ranjan returned from a trip away from the ashram and saw him outside sitting on a bed. When Ranjan went inside Ramana's room he found Ramana's sleeping body lying down. When he told Ramana, the master replied in his typical way to dismiss any matter involving miraculous powers, "Why didn't you tell me at that time? I could have caught the thief!"

Major Chadwick, a Longtime ashram resident, shared a story that an Indian soldier stationed in Burma (Myanmar) during WWII reported seeing Ramana Maharshi standing beside him during a battle, protecting him from harm. Later, when the soldier visited Ramanasramam, Maharshi recognized him and said, "So you saw me there?" – implying bilocation without any further explanation.

An account from Paul Brunton's *A Search in Secret India* (1934) said that a devotee in Madras (Chennai, ~200 km from Tiruvannamalai) claimed to have seen Ramana Maharshi walking near the Kapaleeshwarar Temple while giving spiritual advice. Meanwhile, other devotees at Ramanasramam in Tiruvannamalai confirmed that Maharshi had never left his usual seat in the hall. When asked about it, Ramana simply smiled and said: "Where am I not? The Self is everywhere."

In *The Power of the Presence,* author David Godman recounted the story that a European seeker meditating in his home in Switzerland suddenly "saw" Ramana Maharshi sitting before him, radiating peace. At the same time, devotees in Ramanasramam saw Maharshi deep in meditation on his usual couch. The Swiss seeker later traveled to India and confirmed the exact timing with ashram records. Ramana dismissed the visitor's story lightly: "If you think of me intensely, where else can I be but with you?"

The *Haricharitramrut Sagar* records that in one account, devotees in Vadtal and Gadhada (over 100 km apart) both swore that **Swaminarayan** (1781-1830), the founder of the Swaminarayan Sampradaya, was personally conducting rituals in their temple at the same time. When priests compared notes, they realized it was impossible – yet neither group was lying. Swaminarayan dismissed questions, saying: "Does the sun not shine everywhere at once?"

From oral tradition and devotee testimonies there is a story that a group of dacoits (possibly including figures like Joban Pagi in folklore) planned to loot the Vadtal Temple at night. As they approached, each thief saw Swaminarayan himself standing guard at every entrance – despite witnesses confirming he was asleep in his quarters. Terrified at the multilocation, the thieves fled. The next day, they surrendered and became devotees. When asked, Swaminarayan said: "Where my devotees need protection, I am present in countless forms."

Sri Ramakrishna (1836-1886), the revered 19th-century Hindu mystic and saint, is said to have demonstrated bilocation regularly as part of his advanced yogic powers. When questioned about bilocation, Ramakrishna often dismissed it with metaphors: "When you think of God intensely, He comes to you – why not a man?" or "The body is like a lamp. The flame can be seen in many mirrors at once."

One time he appeared to devotees in Kolkata while meditating in Dakshineswar. The story goes that one evening, Keshab Chandra Sen (a prominent Brahmo Samaj leader) was discussing Ramakrishna with friends in Kolkata when the saint suddenly appeared in their midst, gave spiritual advice, and vanished. Later, when Keshab visited Dakshineswar Temple, Ramakrishna casually remarked, "Did you enjoy our talk last night?"- confirming he had never physically left his room.

At another time, a group of Ramakrishna's disciples traveling to Varanasi claimed they saw him walking beside their boat on the Ganges, guiding them. When they returned to Dakshineswar, Ramakrishna smiled and said, "Yes, I was with you. The body is here, but the mind can wander."

In another instance, a devotee named Girish Chandra Ghosh (playwright) lay critically ill in Kolkata. His family swore they saw Ramakrishna sitting by his bedside, placing a hand on his forehead. Simultaneously, temple records show Ramakrishna was conducting evening *arati* (worship) in Dakshineswar. When Girish recovered and asked Ramakrishna about it, the saint replied, "Does a mother need permission to comfort her child?"

During Ramakrishna's final days, a bread seller in his hometown Kamarpukur (miles from Dakshineswar) claimed the saint bought food from him daily. When villagers checked, Ramakrishna was bedridden and unable to move. Yet, the seller insisted, "He pays me in ash from his pipe!" – a known habit of Ramakrishna.

JUDAISM

Rabbi Isaac Luria (1534-1572), the revered "Ari HaKadosh" or "Holy Lion," was perhaps the most influential Kabbalistic master of the 16th century whose revolutionary system of mystical thought is still studied worldwide today. Beyond his teachings, numerous eyewitness accounts recorded in Kabbalistic texts and oral traditions describe his ability to be in multiple places at once, which is bilocation or multilocation.

The *Shivchei HaAri* (Praises of the Ari) records how two separate disciples in Safed (Tzfat) both invited the master to their homes for the festive meal. Both later testified that he had attended their tables, lead prayers and shared profound wisdom at both locations simultaneously. When confronted with this impossibility, the Ari simply smiled and said: "The soul of a *tzaddik* (righteous man) can be in many places at once."

The *Toldot HaAri* (Biography of the Ari) records a story that a student once saw the Ari immersing in the *mikveh* (ritual bath) at dawn, but when he returned to the study hall, the Ari was already there, fully dressed and teaching. The student asked how this was possible, and the Ari replied: "What you saw was my *nefesh* (lower soul) purifying itself, while my ruach (higher soul) was already in study." As we will later see, this is referring to two types of spiritual bodies.

The *Oral Traditions of Safed* describe mourners in Jerusalem who clearly identified the Ari leading funeral prayers – while his students in Safed (miles away) insisted he had never left their city.

From the *Sefer HaGilgulim* (Book of Reincarnations) is the story that before moving to Safed, the Ari lived in Egypt multiple credible witnesses reported seeing him in different locations simultaneously. A merchant there once swore he saw the Ari studying Kabbalah in an alleyway, while others saw him meditating by the Nile at the same moment.

The Ari's abilities were understood through Lurianic teachings on Soul *Partzufim* ("Divine Faces"), which maintain that a *tzaddik's* soul can manifest through multiple spiritual "layers." Later we'll see this means that an enlightened individual has access to multiple spiritual bodies residing on different planes of existence, which are the multiple spiritual *layers* that the Ari mentioned.

The **Rabbi Israel ben Eliezer** (18th century, Ukraine), known as the **Baal Shem Tov** or the Besht, is the revered founder of Hasidism. He was widely believed to possess supernatural abilities, including the capability of bilocation. There are meticulously recorded accounts of his apparent ability to manifest physically in multiple locations simultaneously, especially to disciples in distant towns while physically elsewhere. These stories are passed down in Hasidic oral tradition and recorded in texts like *Shivchei HaBesht* (In Praise of the Baal Shem Tov).

In the *Shivchei HaBesht* (1814) is one story about a poor couple in Medzhybizh (the Baal Shem Tov's hometown) who invited him to their wedding, but he declined, saying he was needed elsewhere. That same night, a wealthy family in Brody (over 200 km away) insisted he had officiated their son's wedding, even signing the *ketubah* (marriage contract). When the Brody family sent a delegation to thank him, the Baal Shem Tov showed them the identical *ketubah* – despite never physically traveling.

The Chernobyl Hasidim have an oral tradition that a Jewish man imprisoned in Kyiv prayed for the Baal Shem Tov's help. Suddenly, the Besht appeared in his cell, whispering, "Fast tomorrow, and you'll be freed." The next day, the prisoner was miraculously released. When he traveled to Medzhybizh to thank the Besht, disciples said he had been leading a *tisch* (festive meal) the entire time.

From a Breslov tradition, on a Friday evening, women in Tulchin and Sharhorod (50 km apart) both swore the Baal Shem Tov had visited their homes to bless their Sabbath candles. When their husbands compared stories, the Besht laughed and said: "The light of Shabbat is infinite – can one man not share it in many places?"

The *Keter Shem Tov* records the story of a terminally ill merchant in Odessa who saw the Baal Shem Tov at his bedside, holding his hand as he passed, while simultaneously being observed in deep prayer by his students in Medzhybizh.

These accounts aren't mere folklore – they are part of a carefully preserved tradition with consistent details across multiple sources spanning generations. What makes these testimonials so compelling isn't just their consistency but their specificity: exact locations, named witnesses, and precise times that could have been easily disputed by contemporaries had they been fabricated.

Hasidism explains that Baal Shem Tov's bilocation was understood through the doctrine of *Hishtalshelut ha-Neshamot* ("Descent of Souls"), which maintains that a *tzaddik's* soul can fragment to assist others. In Buddhist teachings this represents the *nirmanakaya* abilities of an enlightened sage or Arhat, who can split off multiple copies of his body and condense or "contract" their energy into physical forms that people can see and touch, which Hasidism then calls *Tzimtzum Keli* ("Vessel Contraction"). Hence like the Ari, he could "contract" the split off segments of his transcendental body – which Buddhism calls projections emanations or *nirmanakaya* – into multiple forms.

ISLAM

Multiple historical accounts claim **Abdul Qadir Gilani (Jilani)** (11th–12th century, Baghdad), founder of the Sufi Qadiriyya Order, was seen simultaneously leading prayers in Baghdad and preaching in Mecca. These weren't mere rumors but detailed testimonies from respected community members who had no reason to fabricate such extraordinary claims.

Perhaps the most compelling evidence comes from Gilani's brief imprisonment. While guards believed they had confined the saint in his cell, his devoted disciples reported seeing him leading prayers in Baghdad. When authorities rushed to his cell to investigate this impossibility, they found him deep in prayer – yet inexplicably, his fresh footprints were found on the ground outside the prison.

Ibn al-ʿArabi (1165-1240), the renowned Andalusian Sufi mystic and philosopher, is celebrated in Islam for his profound metaphysical teachings and spiritual experiences. Abd al-Wahhab al-Sha'rani compiled forty accounts of his bilocation in *Al-Yawaqit wa al-Jawahir*.

From *Al-Futuhat al-Makkiyya* (The Meccan Revelations) we have the story that Ibn Arabi's disciples in Damascus reported him delivering a lecture on divine love *('ishq)* in the Umayyad Mosque. At the same time, pilgrims in Mecca swore they saw him performing *tawaf* (circumambulation of the Kaaba). When questioned, he replied: "The heart of the gnostic *('arif)* is with God, and God is everywhere."

The *Nafh al-Tib* by Al-Maqqari reports the story of a revered scholar who died in Aleppo (Syria), and Ibn Arabi was seen leading the funeral prayer. That same hour, mourners in Seville (Spain) – his birthplace – also claimed he presided over their rites. He later explained: "The body is a shadow; the Real *(al-Haqq)* has no location."

Lastly, Oral Tradition from Moroccan Sufis relate that the Sultan of Fez once summoned Ibn Arabi to court, only to find him simultaneously feeding the poor in a beggar's hut outside the city. When courtiers rushed to the hut, Ibn Arabi was gone – yet the beggar testified he had just left. The Sultan, humbled, became his disciple.

Ahmed ar-Rifa'i (12th century, Iraq), the founder of the Rifa'iyya Sufi order, led a life replete with accounts of extraordinary spiritual experiences and miracles. Hafiz Muhaddith Abul Farj Wasti Shafi'i notes in his spiritual treatise, titled as *Tiryaq al-Muhibbin fi Tabaqat Kharqah al-Mashaikh al-Arifin* (An Antidote for Divine Lovers in the circle of Wise Sages): "Sayyid Ahmad Kabir Rifai is considered the Imam of *Mashaikhs* (Sufi saints) and the Sultan of his time as well as the leader of Awliya and Ahlul-Allah (God's friends) of his age. Certainly, we did not find anyone of the spiritual stature of Syed Ahmad Rifai after the 12 Imams of *Ahlul-Bayt* (Prophet's household) and *Sahabas* (Prophet's companions). In terms of creation *(Khalqat)*, spiritual authority *(Tariqat)*, realisation of Truth *(Haqiqat)* and possession of Gnosis *(Ma'rifat)*, he was an embodiment of divinity *(Rabbaniyat)* who walked properly in the footsteps of his ancestor, the Holy Prophet (peace and blessings be upon him)."

Ar-Rifa is renowned for his extraordinary spiritual powers *(karamat)*, including bilocation. He was said to have appeared to multiple people in different cities during times of need His miracles are documented in classical Sufi texts like *Bahjat al-Asrar* and *Tabaqat al-Kubra*. Here are some of the most famous accounts:

The *Bahjat al-Asrar* (The Joy of Secrets) recounts that Sheikh ar-Rifa'i was seen leading the Friday prayer at the Great Mosque. In Basra (Iraq), At the exact same time, villagers in Umm 'Ubayda (a distant Iraqi town) swore he was leading their congregation in a small masjid.

From *Tabaqat al-Kubra by as-Sha'rani there is the story of* a dying man in Wasit (Iraq) who cried out for ar-Rifa'i's help. The saint appeared, placed his hand on the man's forehead, and healed him. That same hour, a woman in Baghdad claimed ar-Rifa'i had visited her sick child, leaving a mark of rosewater on the child's brow. When witnesses compared stories, they found the same scent of roses on both healed individuals.

An Oral Tradition from Rifa'i Sufis says that the Abbasid Caliph once invited ar-Rifa'i to a royal banquet in Baghdad. While the nobles saw him seated at the table, beggars outside the palace gates swore he was feeding them with his own hands. When the Caliph sent guards to check, they found scraps of food matching the palace feast – but ar-Rifa'i never physically left the banquet.

Shams Tabrizi (13th century, Persia), the enigmatic spiritual master and mentor of **Rumi** (1207-1273), was renowned for his miraculous abilities, including bilocation. Shams was infamous for disappearing suddenly and reappearing miles away, which are classic descriptions of bilocation.

One evening in Konya, Shams was seen deep in conversation with Rumi in a mosque. The next morning, a merchant from Damascus arrived, claiming he had just spoken with Shams in the Umayyad Mosque – over 600 km away – where Shams had given him a cryptic spiritual lesson. When confronted, Shams replied: "The body is a shadow. The sun (Shams) can cast its light wherever it wishes."

Recorded in Sultan Walad's (Rumi's son) writings is the story of a time a disciple swore he saw Shams leading Friday prayers at the Kaaba in Mecca, while others in Konya simultaneously witnessed him teaching in Rumi's courtyard. When skeptics demanded proof, Shams lifted his robe to reveal wet footprints from the Kaaba's sacred Zamzam well.

From Aflaki's *Manāqib al-'Ārifīn (Acts of the Gnostics, 14th century).* A drunkard in Aleppo mocked Shams, saying, "If you're such a saint, appear before me tonight!" That night, Shams materialized in the man's room, causing him to repent. Meanwhile, Rumi's students saw Shams meditating undisturbed in Konya.

One of the most celebrated bilocation stories in Sufi tradition revolves around **Sheikh Abu al-Fadl al-Hadithi** (d. late 19th century), a mystic from Iraq known for his spiritual insights, miraculous abilities (*karamat*), and devotion to the Hadithi-Qadiri order, which is a branch of the Qadiriyya tariqa emphasizing hadith scholarship alongside Sufi practice. Sheikh al-Fadl's legacy persists in Iraqi Sufi circles, where he is remembered for bilocation and instantaneous travel (*tayy al-makan*), healing the sick through spiritual presence, and dream-visitations guiding disciples long after his death. Although details vary across oral accounts, the core bilocation narrative of his abilities describes him teaching simultaneously in Lebanon and Syria on the same day – a miracle (*karama*) that cemented his status as a Qutb (spiritual axis) of his time.

A famous story runs that one Friday, disciples in Damascus, Syria, gathered for his weekly *dhikr* (remembrance of God) and Quranic discourse. That same afternoon, villagers in Mount Lebanon (over 100 km away) swore they had attended a Sufi gathering where Sheikh al-Fadel gave a passionate sermon on divine love *('ishq)*. When Lebanese travelers later visited Damascus and mentioned the sheikh's lecture, the Syrian disciples were stunned – he had never left their mosque. Each group described him wearing different clothes but the same ring. This tale survives in oral histories of the Hadithi-Qadiri Sufi order and is recounted in *Tales of the Awliya* (Nur al-Din al-Hadithi, 1923).

There are also accounts of the famous Indian Sufi saint, **Shirdi Sai Baba** (1838-1918), exhibiting the phenomenon of bilocation, wherein he appeared in multiple places simultaneously to assist his devotees.

One notable instance is documented in the *Shri Sai Satcharitra*, the revered biography of Sai Baba. In this account, a devotee named Balram Mankar, residing in Macchindragad (District Satara, Maharashtra), experienced a profound vision. While deeply engrossed in meditation, he perceived Sai Baba standing before him in tangible form. This occurred while Sai Baba was physically present in Shirdi, approximately 300 kilometers away. This event is considered a classic example of Sai Baba's bilocation, where he extended his spiritual presence to guide and comfort a devotee in need.

In another instance, a devotee named Nana Saheb Chandorkar was serving as a government officer in Mamlatdar's Court (Thane district, Maharashtra) while also frequently visiting Shirdi. One day, while Nana was at work, Sai Baba physically appeared before him, spoke to him, and even handed him a piece of fruit (a banana or an orange, depending on retellings). At the exact same time, multiple devotees in Shirdi swore that Sai Baba was sitting in the Dwarkamai Mosque, holding conversations and distributing food. When Nana later returned to Shirdi, Sai Baba confirmed the event by asking, "Did you enjoy the fruit I gave you?"

A young boy, the son of a devotee, was drowning in a river in Nagpur (hundreds of kilometers from Shirdi). The boy later testified that an "old fakir with a white beard" (Sai Baba) pulled him out of the water. At the same time, devotees in Shirdi saw Sai Baba sitting in his usual place, completely dry. When the boy's family traveled to Shirdi to thank Baba, he simply smiled and said, "You recognized me, that's good."

A wealthy merchant in Bombay (now Mumbai) was on his deathbed and desperately wished to see Sai Baba one last time. Suddenly, Sai Baba appeared at his bedside, blessed him, and gave him *udhi* (sacred ash). The merchant recovered and later traveled to Shirdi to thank Baba, only to find that he had never left the village that day. When questioned, Baba simply said, "You called, so I came."

A devotee named Bapusaheb Booty was involved in a legal dispute in Aurangabad. During the trial, the opposing lawyer suddenly saw Sai Baba standing behind Booty, intimidating him into silence. Meanwhile, in Shirdi, Baba was seen grinding wheat in the Dwarkamai Mosque. When Booty returned to Shirdi, Baba joked, "Did my presence in court help you?"

Sai Baba would often perform night processions (Chavadi processions) where he would ceremonially move between the mosque and the Chavadi building. Some devotees reported seeing him both in the procession and simultaneously sitting in the mosque. When questioned, Baba would laugh and say, "I am where my devotees need me."

BAHAI FAITH

The **Báb** (1819–1850), born **Siyyid ʿAlí-Muḥammad**, was the prophet-herald of the Baháʾí faith. While imprisoned in Maku (1847–1848) and later Chihriq, disciples in distant cities (such as Shiraz and Isfahan) reported seeing him in their midst while he was confirmed as incarcerated in prison. Guards and officials swore he never left his cell, yet devotees testified to receiving guidance from him physically during this time.

Followers in Shiraz and Tabriz also independently reported that the Báb led them in prayer on the same night while he was known to be detained in a remote fortress. Some described him handing them sacred verses in person, which matched writings he later produced in prison.

SIKHISM

In the *Janamsakhis*, there are multiple biographical stories of **Guru Nanak Dev Ji** (15th–16th century), founder of Sikhism, appearing in two places at once. The most famous example was when he was seen simultaneously praying in Mecca while also teaching in Punjab. According to the Puratan Janamsakhi, while in Mecca he lay down to sleep with his feet pointed toward the Kaaba, angering the local *qazis* (Islamic judges), who accused him of disrespect. When the *qazis* tried to forcibly move his feet, they witnessed the Kaaba itself rotating to align with Guru Nanak's feet, symbolizing the omnipresence of the Divine. Simultaneously, Sikh devotees in Kartarpur (Punjab) reported seeing Guru Nanak teaching and leading kirtan (devotional singing) at the exact same time.

In the Bhai Bala Janamsakhi, villagers in Sayyidpur (now Eminabad, Pakistan) and Achal Batala (Punjab) claimed Guru Nanak was personally guiding them on the same day, despite the distance.

During his travels (*udasis*), he was said to manifest in distant locations to guide seekers.

Guru Gobind Singh Ji (17th–18th century), the tenth guru of Sikhism, performed bilocation during the midst of a battle. During the siege of Anandpur Sahib, one of the most harrowing battles in Sikh history, some soldiers claimed to see Guru Gobind Singh fighting on the front lines leading the charge while simultaneously meditating in his tent undisturbed by the battle's fury.

For **Sant Baba Ishar Singh Ji** (1905-1975), a revered Brahmgiani Sikh saint from Rara Sahib and spiritual successor to **Sant Baba Attar Singh Ji Mastuane Wale** (1866-1927), there are reports from disciples seeing him blessing devotees in India while physically residing in his monastery. Disciples claimed to have seen Baba Ishar Singh Ji giving darshan (divine sight) and offering blessings at Gurdwaras in Amritsar, Patiala, or even abroad, while others confirmed he was never physically absent from Rara Sahib. In some cases, devotees who received his blessings at distant locations later visited Rara Sahib, only to be told by sevadars (servants) that he had not left the premises that day.

There are accounts of gravely ill or dying Sikhs seeing Baba Ishar Singh Ji at their bedside, comforting them and reciting Gurbani, while his physical body remained in meditation at Rara Sahib.

A famous incident describes a shortage of food during a large gathering at Rara Sahib. Baba Ishar Singh Ji was seen supervising the langar in person, yet simultaneously, devotees in another city saw him distributing prasad (blessed food) to the needy.

SHUGENDO

In Shugendo, the Japanese mountain ascetic tradition blending Esoteric Buddhism (Mikkyo), Shinto, and Taoist-influenced practices, advanced practitioners (*yamabushi* or *shugenja*) were believed to attain supernatural abilities (*siddhi* or *jinzū*) through rigorous asceticism (*shugyō*). Among these powers, bilocation as the projection of tangible spiritual bodies (analogous to what Chinese Taoists call the *yang-shen*) appears in legends and esoteric texts. Below are two examples:

Legends say **En no Gyoja** (7th-8th century), the founder of Shugendo, could appear simultaneously at Kumano Shrines (in Wakayama) and Yoshino peaks (in Nara), separated by over 70 km of rugged mountains. Legends say that during important rituals, En no Gyoja would manifest physically at both locations at once, conducting ceremonies simultaneously. Witnesses at both sites reported seeing, hearing, and interacting with him as if he were fully present.

When exiled to Izu Oshima, an island south of Edo (modern Tokyo), after being accused of "using magic to manipulate people," he was also said to have projected his presence back to Yamato to continue teaching during his physical banishment. Authorities, baffled by reports of his presence on the mainland, investigated only to find him still confined on the island.

JAINISM

The Scriptures of Jainism mention cases of **Mahavira** (6th century BC), the 24th Tirthankara, performing the act of bilocation. The *Acharanga Sutra* and *Kalpa Sutra* describe Mahavira preaching to multiple audiences at once through this form of divine projection. It reports that while meditating in a forest, Mahavira was sought by multiple groups of disciples in distant locations. Instead of traveling conventionally, he projected his presence to each group, allowing them to see and hear him as if he were physically there.

During a grand assembly at Rajagriha, Mahavira was teaching King Shrenika when devotees in Vaisali and Kundagrama also reported seeing and hearing him. His voice and form were simultaneously perceptible in multiple places, a phenomenon called "spiritual expansion" (*samudghāta*) in Jainism.

Gautama Swami (6th century BC), chief disciple of Mahavira, is also mentioned in *The Uttaradhyayana Sutra* teaching in multiple locations during Mahavira's final sermon. While Mahavira was preaching, Gautama Swami was seen simultaneously in different locations, delivering discourses to different groups of disciples so that multiple assemblies could receive his guidance at the same time. This proved his worthiness as a succor to Mahavira. When questioned about this miracle, Gautama Swami reportedly attributed it to his mastery over the Jain spiritual disciplines (*gunasthana*). He explained that a purified soul, free from karmic obstructions, can manifest in multiple forms to serve living beings.

TAOISM

In Taoism, bilocation is often associated with *yang-shen* abilities where an accomplished Taoist spiritual master, who is called an "immortal" (*xian*), can project their spirit across distances whereupon it can then coalesce into a tangible physical form. It's a spiritual attainment one achieves after years of meditation and internal energy cultivation practice. The stories of these abilities appear in Taoist hagiographies, internal alchemy texts, and oral lineages. Some of the famous individuals known for bilocation powers include the following:

Lu Dongbin (Tang dynasty 8th–9th century), a central figure in Taoist lore, was said to appear in multiple places simultaneously – teaching disciples, aiding the needy, and even appearing in dreams. In the *Zhong-Lü Chuan Dao Ji*, Lu Dongbin and his teacher Zhongli Quan demonstrate "appearing and disappearing at will."

In *The Eight Immortals Attain the Dao*, there is a story about a wealthy merchant in Luoyang who hosted a grand banquet, inviting Lu Dongbin as an honored guest. At the same time, a poor scholar in Hangzhou also claimed to have dined with Lu Dongbin, who gifted him a magical poem predicting his future success. When the two men later met and compared stories, they realized Lu Dongbin had been at both banquets simultaneously.

The *Lü Zu Quanshu* records the story that a swordsman in Wudang Mountain sought Lu Dongbin's teachings and saw him practicing sword forms at sunrise. That same morning, monks at Mount Hua also reported receiving sword instruction from him. When the swordsman traveled to Mount Hua, the monks confirmed the timing – Lu Dongbin had been in both places at once.

In another instance, *The Records of the Eight Immortals* says that while meditating on Mount Lu, Lu Dongbin was simultaneously seen healing the sick in a distant village.

From *The Drunken Immortal* is the story that one evening, patrons at two different wine shops in Yueyang City swore he was drinking and reciting verses in their establishments at the same time. When they compared notes, they realized he had never physically moved between them.

Daoist teachings state that Lu Dongbin's abilities stem from *yang-shen chu you* – projecting the "spirit body" while the physical form remains still. The Daoist art of self-duplication is called *fen-shen shu*, and it is achieved after years on inner alchemy practices where one circulates their internal energies around inside themselves.

Lu Dongbin wrote in *The Secret of the Golden Flower*: "The sage is like the moon – one in essence, but reflected in ten thousand waters."

Zhang Sanfeng (c. 12th–14th century), the legendary founder of Wudang Mountain Taoism, internal alchemy and master of Taijiquan (Tai Chi), is revered in Chinese folklore for his supernatural abilities, including bilocation (*fen-shen shu*). The stories of his abilities reinforce the Taoist teachings that internal alchemy exercises (*neidan, neijia* or *nei-gong*) eventually enable physical bilocation. His *Taiji Neigong* practices were said to cultivate a physical spirit-body that could travel beyond the physical form, showing that he had achieved *yang-shen* mastery, namely the power of bilocation that comes from achieving a certain stage of sainthood.

Though historical records are sparse, Ming Dynasty texts and oral traditions preserve astonishing tales of his simultaneous manifestations. These records claim Zhang Sanfeng was seen teaching martial arts in Wudang Mountain while also appearing in Sichuan on the same day.

From *Zhang Sanfeng's Complete Works* (Ming Dynasty) there is a story of students training on Wudang Mountain with Zhang Sanfeng in Taiji sword forms at dawn. That same morning, monks on Emei Mountain (over 1,000 km away) claimed he was teaching Qigong in their monastery.

A story recorded in *Unofficial History of the Ming Dynasty* is that the Hongwu Emperor (r. 1368–1398) sent envoys to Wudang to summon Zhang Sanfeng to court. They found him meditating in a cave. Simultaneously, villagers in Shaanxi reported sharing a meal with a ragged beggar who revealed himself as Zhang – before vanishing mid-bite. The envoys returned to the emperor empty-handed, but the beggar's description matched Zhang perfectly.

A folktale from *Legends of the Inner Alchemy Masters* relates that a bandit in Kaifeng challenged Zhang Sanfeng to a fight, only to see him draw a sword and vanish. At the same time, a magistrate in Nanjing witnessed Zhang subduing a corrupt official with the same sword techniques. The bandit, shaken, abandoned violence and became a monk.

From Wudang oral tradition there is a story that during a blizzard, shepherds near Mount Hua saw Zhang Sanfeng walking barefoot in the snow, guiding them to shelter. Meanwhile, his disciples in Wudang swore he had been meditating in his hut for days without leaving. When asked, he wrote a poem: "Above the peaks, one body; In the valleys, ten thousand shadows."

Wang Chongyang, the legendary founder of Quanzhen (Complete

Reality) Taoism, was renowned for his spiritual powers, including bilocation (*fenshen shu*). While historical records focus on his teachings, Ming Dynasty Taoist texts and Quanzhen oral traditions preserve remarkable accounts of his simultaneous manifestations. After his supposed death, he appeared to disciples in a solid, tangible form to give final teachings.

The *Quanzhen Annals* describes him materializing in multiple locations posthumously.

Recorded in *Legends of the Seven Quanzhen Masters*, beggars in Xi'an swore Wang Chongyang personally fed them rice from his bowl one winter night. Simultaneously, his senior disciple Ma Yu saw him meditating in Shandong, never leaving his hut.

A folktale from *Wondrous Records of Quanzhen* reports that a village near Huashan was plagued by evil spirits. Villagers saw Wang Chongyang performing an exorcism at midnight. At the exact same hour, his disciples in Henan witnessed him calmly writing scriptures in their temple. The next day, both groups found identical talismans – one used in the exorcism, the other freshly inked.

From *Ming Dynasty Court Records* there is a story that the Jin Dynasty Emperor sent guards to summon Wang to court. They found him drinking tea in a Kaifeng tavern. Yet palace attendants insisted he'd been meditating in the imperial garden the whole time.

Wang's abilities stem from cultivating both nature and life-force (one's Qi) to achieve mastery of inner alchemy, as taught in his *Ganshui Xianyuan Lu*. With mastery of the stages of cultivation, one could then project the "spirit body" while the physical form remains still.

ANCIENT AND MEDIEVAL RELIGIOUS FIGURES

The ancient Greek philosopher **Pythagoras** (c. 570–490 BC) was said to have been capable of bilocation. According to Porphyry (writing several centuries after Pythagoras): Almost unanimous is the report that on one and the same day Pythagoras was present at Metapontum in Italy, and at Tauromenium in Sicily, in each place conversing with his friends, though the places are separated by many miles, both at sea and land, demanding many days' journey.

A similar story is told of **Apollonius of Tyana** (15-98), one of the most famous spiritual teachers and miracle workers during a period of the

Roman Empire, was reported by witnesses as present simultaneously in Smyrna and Ephesus.

The story goes that Apollonius was in Smyrna (modern-day İzmir, Turkey) when he received word that a deadly plague had broken out in Ephesus (about 50 km away). The Ephesians begged him to come and save them, believing his divine wisdom could stop the disease. Rather than travel normally, Apollonius announced: "Let us go to the theater in Ephesus." He then instantly appeared in Ephesus, where he identified an old beggar as the "demon of the plague." He commanded the Ephesians to stone the beggar, and when they did, the plague ceased.

Remarkably, witnesses in Smyrna claimed Apollonius was still among them at the same time he was seen in Ephesus. Philostratus writes that people in both cities swore they had seen and spoken with him during the event. When questioned about how he accomplished this, Apollonius cryptically replied: "I was present with you, but I also saw what was happening in Ephesus."

Albertus Magnus (c. 1200–1280), also known as Saint Albert the Great, was a Dominican friar, theologian, philosopher, and scientist renowned for his vast knowledge in natural philosophy, alchemy, and theology. A teacher of Thomas Aquinas, he was one of the most learned men of the Middle Ages and was later canonized as a saint by the Catholic Church.

Dominican chronicles report that Albertus was once invited to a grand banquet by a nobleman or bishop. However, he was simultaneously expected to attend a solemn religious ceremony at his monastery. Rather than choosing one event over the other, Albertus miraculously appeared at both – fully present in each location – fulfilling his obligations in a supernatural manner. He appeared simultaneously in Cologne and Paris.

Paracelsus (1493–1541), a Swiss alchemist, physician and mystic, gave spiritual teachings that were deeply rooted in Hermeticism, Neoplatonism, and Christian mysticism. Paracelsus proposed that an invisible vital force (archeus) governed health and disease, which was basically the Indian idea of Prana and the Chinese Taoist idea of Qi, or life force. By aligning with one's inner life force through alchemy, prayer, and natural medicine one could restore harmony to one's body and eventually transmute the soul into divine perfection.

Paracelsus was surrounded by legends of supernatural abilities. He reportedly predicted future events, including his own death (which, according to legend, he foretold would happen shortly after a fatal ambush by assassins). He allegedly cured "incurable" diseases, including cases of leprosy and plague, and is said to have healed patients in Nuremberg while physically in Basel. In *De Vita Longa*, he describes the "sidereal body" (*astrum*) – a tangible spiritual form that could travel independently that is the source of bilocation.

BUDDHISM

In Hindu and Buddhist traditions, bilocation is considered one of the siddhi, or supernatural powers that can be developed through devoted spiritual practices. In the Digha Nikaya (Long Discourses of the Buddha), King Ajatasattu asks the Buddha about the fruits of the monastic life, whereupon the Buddha describes the supernormal powers (*siddhi*) attainable through deep meditation, including the capability of multiplying the body, and vanishing and reappearing at will, which pertain to bilocation or multilocation.

Shakyamuni Buddha (c. 500 BC) himself is said to have demonstrated the ability to instantly travel great distances. In one account, he vanished from the Deer Park (Sarnath) and instantly reappeared in front of his disciple Anuruddha, who needed guidance at the time, in a different location. The Buddha was teaching at Deer Park (Sarnath) when he sensed his disciple Anuruddha (elsewhere, possibly in Kosambi or Jetavana) needed guidance. This was not merely a vision – Anuruddha and others present saw and interacted with the Buddha physically.

In Buddhist traditions, particularly within Mahayana, Vajrayana, and Chan (Zen) Buddhism, there are many accounts of advanced monks and masters demonstrating extraordinary abilities, including bilocation with tangible emanations (*yang-shen*) – a phenomenon described in Taoism and Esoteric Buddhism. In Buddhism, the tangible *yang-shen* is either a *nirmanakaya* emanation (*hua-shen*), or a higher spiritual body (not an emanation or projection) belonging to the stage of an Arhat or higher, that condenses the energies around itself so that it can become a visible, tangible form.

As seen, bilocation is one of the Six Supernatural Powers in Buddhism, so information about it appears in Chinese Buddhist texts, particularly in biographies of eminent monks. These Six Supernatural Powers are advanced spiritual attainments that result from deep meditation practice, and are mentioned in Theravada, Mahayana, and Vajrayana texts, including the *Samannaphala Sutta* (DN 2) and the *Mahaprajnaparamita Sastra*.

The Six Supernatural Powers include (1) the Divine Eye that gives one the ability to see past, future, and distant events (including rebirths of beings), (2) the Divine Ear that gives one the ability to hear sounds from any distance, (3) Mind Reading, which gives one the ability to know others' thoughts and emotions, (4) Recollection of Past Lives where one can remember one's own and others' past lives in detail, (5) Supernatural Powers that include Bilocation (being in multiple places at once), walking on water, flying, invisibility, materializing objects, and control over elements (fire, water, etc.), and (6) Extinction of Mental Defilements, which means the destruction of all cravings so as to attain ultimate liberation.

Many of these powers are also seen in the cases of Christian saints, such as mind reading and of course bilocation, which is our topic of investigation. Bilocation appears in many Buddhist texts, particularly in biographies of eminent monks, and in the accounts of accomplished Buddhist masters from every one of its traditions. Below are some of the most notable cases:

According to legend, **Hui Neng** (638-713), the Sixth Patriarch of Zen, once appeared in two places at the same time – he remained in his meditation seat and was simultaneously seen giving teachings elsewhere in another monastery. He demonstrated what Chan Buddhism (Zen) speaks of as "transformation bodies" (*hua-shen*), also called *nirmanakaya*, where adepts project physical or energy forms. His uncorrupted body currently resides at Nanhua Temple in Guangdong where he taught for thirty-seven years.

The *Biographies of Eminent Monks* records that **Fazang** (643–712), a Buddhist master of the Huayan school, was publicly giving a lecture in Chang'an (the imperial capital) while simultaneously manifesting on Wutai Mountain – a distance of hundreds of miles – where he was seen by multiple witness, including monks and nuns. On multiple occasions his

INCORRUPTIBLE BODIES AND BILOCATION MIRACLES

prayers and rites would bring rain to regions of drought.

A monk reported seeing **Hanshan** (9th Century), the eccentric poet-hermit, both meditating in a cave and begging for food in a distant village on the same day.

Transmission of the Lamp records that Zen master **Mazu Daoyi** (709–788), founder of the Hongzhou school of Zen, was seen by disciples teaching in Jiangxi while also appearing in Fujian, with both groups recalling identical sermons.

Records of the Transmission of the Lamp states that After his supposed death, a Chinese official reported meeting **Bodhidharma** (5th–6th Century), the legendary Chan Patriarch, walking barefoot in the mountains of Central Asia – after being buried in China where his tomb remained sealed.

Folk legends claim **Jigong** (1130–1209), the Mad Monk of Hangzhou, attended banquets in multiple cities at once, leaving behind his signature tattered hat as proof. He purportedly possessed supernatural powers through Buddhist practice, and many stories relate that Jigong used his superpowers to help the poor and stand up to injustice. In one popular story, Ji Gong was helping construct a temple in Hangzhou City. When they ran out of lumber, he began teleporting logs from a forest in Sichuan province, some 900 miles away. The massive logs just started shooting out of a well one by one, like some magical lumber portal. The story is significant because in many cases of bilocation, a master can carry objects with him.

From the *Blue Cliff Record, Case 16*, Zen master **Yunmen Wenyan** (864–949) once answered a question in the meditation hall while also being seen crossing a river outside the monastery.

In his autobiography, disciples claimed **Hsu Yun** (1840–1959), a modern Chan (Zen) master, attended a lecture in Shanghai while in deep meditation at a mountain temple. Hsu Yun was known to be able to close his eyes and would not talk, eat, or drink, and stayed in the samadhi for nine days while his attendants Fayun and Kuanchun waited on him.

The founder of the Dhammakaya Buddhist tradition in Thailand, **Luang Pu Sodh Candasaro** (1884-1959), was said to have appeared to disciples in multiple places at once, a phenomenon recorded by his followers. There are many stories of his ability to perform bilocation by projecting a body double.

From *The Life of Luang Pu Sodh* (Wat Paknam Bhasicharoen archives) there is the story that one evening, monks at Wat Paknam Bhasicharoen (Bangkok) saw Luang Pu Sodh leading a meditation session in the main hall. At the same time, villagers in Wat Phra Dhammakaya (Pathum Thani) swore he was giving a Dharma talk there. When disciples compared notes, they realized he had not traveled between temples.

An oral tradition from senior monks is that a sick devotee in Chiang Mai prayed for Luang Pu Sodh's blessing. That night, he saw the monk enter his room, place a hand on his head, and vanish. The next morning, the man traveled to Wat Paknam to thank him – only to learn Luang Pu Sodh had been in Bangkok the entire time, hosting visitors.

In the 1940s, Thai Royal Court Officials (1940s) reported that during a royal merit-making ceremony, officials saw Luang Pu Sodh seated among the monks in Bangkok's Grand Palace. Meanwhile, farmers in Ayutthaya (80 km away) claimed he walked through their fields, blessing their crops. Palace attendants confirmed he never left the ceremony.

From disciples' memoirs there is the case that one morning, laypeople in Nakhon Pathom offered food to Luang Pu Sodh during his alms round. That same morning, devotees in Samut Prakan also gave alms to him. Both groups later met and realized he couldn't have been in both places physically.

In Vajrayana Buddhism, bilocation is linked to *siddhis* (spiritual powers) attained through tantric practice, and has been reported of many modern monks in Tibet, Nepal, Bhutan and Sikkim. Several famous Tibetan practitioners known for bilocation include:

Yeshe Tsogyal (8th Century), the consort of Padmasambhava, was reported to appear to multiple disciples in different locations to give teachings while remaining in retreat.

Milarepa (11th–12th century), the great Tibetan yogi, was seen by a disciple meditating in a cave while simultaneously appearing in a marketplace begging for food. His student Rechungpa also saw Milarepa simultaneously meditating in his cave and appearing elsewhere to teach Dharma. Milarepa was known for being able to project energy forms (*nirmanakaya*) that interacted with disciples physically.

Rangjung Rigpe Dorje (1924-1981), the 16th Karmapa who is head of the Kagyu school of Tibetan Buddhism, was widely regarded as an enlightened mahasiddha (great yogi with supernatural powers). Among his many attributed miracles, bilocation is one of the most frequently reported. For instance, in the mid-1970s, the Karmapa was residing at Rumtek Monastery in Sikkim, India. At the same time, multiple students in France and Switzerland reported seeing him in their meditation halls or giving blessings – despite no record of him traveling. Some claimed to have received physical objects (blessed threads, relics) from him during these encounters though he never left India.

In another instance, disciples at Tsurphu Monastery (Tibet, pre-1959 exile) and Palpung Monastery (Eastern Tibet) both insisted the Karmapa was personally teaching them on the same day. When questioned, he reportedly laughed and said, "For the Buddha, there is no near or far."

During the Black Crown Ceremony (where the Karmapa manifests as Avalokitesvara), attendees in different countries (USA, India, Nepal) even claimed to see his physical form multiply during the ceremony.

A dying disciple in Calcutta (1980) swore the Karmapa visited his bedside to grant final blessings. Monks at Rumtek later confirmed the Karmapa was in strict retreat that day.

CONCLUSION: THE NON-SECTARIAN PHENOMENON OF BILOCATION

The remarkable cases documented throughout this chapter reveal a profound truth about bilocation: this extraordinary ability transcends religious boundaries, appearing consistently across diverse spiritual traditions throughout human history. From Catholic saints like Padre Pio and Martin de Porres to Hindu yogis like Neem Karoli Baba and Ramana Maharshi, from Taoist immortals like Lu Dongbin to Buddhist masters like the 16th Karmapa – the phenomenon appears with striking similarity across cultures separated by time, geography, and doctrine.

What makes this phenomenon particularly compelling is its appearance in the sacred scriptures and authoritative texts of multiple religions, as well as cases investigated and confirmed by the Catholic Church. Buddhism explicitly includes bilocation among the Six Supernatural Powers attainable through advanced meditation practice. Taoist internal alchemy texts describe the development of the *yang-shen* or "spirit body" capable of tangible materialization, namely bilocation. Jewish Kabbalistic writings reference the ability of a *tzaddik's* soul to manifest through multiple "layers." These textual foundations suggest bilocation is not merely folkloric embellishment but rather an acknowledged non-denominational power available on the advanced spiritual path.

The mechanics of bilocation, while described in different terminologies across traditions, appear remarkably consistent. Whether called *nirmanakaya* emanations in Buddhism, *fen-shen shu* in Taoism, a "layer" of the soul by Rabbi Luria, or an "extension of personality" as Padre Pio described it, the core process involves a spiritually advanced individual projecting energetic copies of themselves that condense into tangible forms that witnesses can see and sometimes even touch. These projections are not mere apparitions or visions but interactive manifestations capable of physical interaction – healing the sick, providing blessings, or delivering teachings or items. As the Rabbi Luria suggested, somehow different "layers" of the soul can manifest simultaneously, but only for spiritually advanced individuals.

Perhaps most telling is the consistent attitude of the saints themselves toward their extraordinary ability. Across traditions, those who demonstrate bilocation typically dismiss questions about it or deflect attention from the phenomenon. When Padre Pio was asked how bilocation worked, he simply described it as an "extension of his personality." When devotees questioned Ramana Maharshi about appearing elsewhere, he humorously suggested he could have "caught the thief." This humility and reluctance to discuss the mechanics reflects a common understanding that such abilities, while real, are merely byproducts of spiritual advancement rather than goals in themselves, and they are not easily explained because people would not understand the mechanics of the achievement.

The non-denominational nature of bilocation suggests it represents a universal aspect of human spiritual potential rather than the exclusive domain of any single faith. The scientific community may dismiss such accounts as impossible according to known physical laws, yet the weight of testimony across cultures – often from reliable, skeptical witnesses – presents a compelling case that the phenomenon is real and that the ladder of spiritual progress may operate by principles not yet fully understood by conventional science. The consistency of these accounts across religious boundaries suggests that bilocation emerges not from theological doctrine but from universal patterns of advanced spiritual development accessible to devoted practitioners of many paths.

What remains clear is that bilocation, while extraordinary, appears consistently as a marker of advanced spiritual attainment. Across traditions, it manifests not among beginners but among those who have devoted decades to rigorous spiritual practice, ethical development, and self-transcendence. The phenomenon thus stands as evidence that the world's diverse spiritual paths, while differing in approach and terminology, may ultimately lead dedicated practitioners to similar transformative heights of spiritual abilities – heights where the conventional limitations of physical existence begin to yield to expanded possibilities of being and service.

CHAPTER 2:
OUR FIVE SPIRITUAL BODIES

How does bilocation happen? Let's first review a few explanations offered by various saints, or their spiritual traditions that comment on the phenomenon.

Rabbi Isaac Luria's bilocation abilities were understood through Lurianic teachings that a *tzaddik's* soul can manifest through multiple spiritual "layers." Hasidism explains that Baal Shem Tov's bilocation abilities were possible because a *tzaddik's* soul can <u>fragment</u> to assist others.

Padre Pio described bilocation as an "extension of his personality." Sri Yukteswar said, "This body is a materialized thought-projection, as real as your own. ... These are not mere reflections like the images of a cinema, but are individualized manifestations of the master's divine *life force*."

Mahavira's bilocation abilities were called "spiritual expansion" in Jainism. According to Taoist metaphysics, bilocation is one of the standard abilities of an accomplished Taoist spiritual master who reaches a certain stage of achievement, and who can then project their spirit across distances and condense it into a physical form after years of internal energy practices called *nei-gong, neidan* or *neijia*.

Taoism calls this ability to project a spirit body *fen-shen shu*. When it assumes tangible form that others can see and touch the projection is then called a *yang-shen* emanation. In *De Vita Longa*, Paracelsus explained that an accomplished spiritual master attains a "sidereal body" or tangible spiritual form that could travel independently, and which is the source of bilocation.

In Buddhist traditions, bilocation is one of the six supernatural powers of all people who achieve spiritual enlightenment, the rank of spiritual liberation, which is why it is seen across all these traditions for spiritual saints and masters. The tangible *yang-shen* is either a *nirmanakaya* energy emanation (*hua-shen*) that is split off from the body of an accomplished master that then condenses itself into form, or it is the higher spiritual body of the master himself that coalesces into form rather than a temporary emanation or projection.

Scientific research has described the ability to project a tangible *yang-shen* as particle-ization (energy to particle transformation), particle manifestation (an energy field becoming observable particles) or particle condensation. These terms describe the process of coalescing spiritual energy into a tangible form and then dissolving it, akin to the bilocation or materialization seen of saints.

An example of the fact that this can even our physical body can be transformed into energy and then recondensed, after years of spiritual cultivation effort when one's practice is high enough, came from the Hindu master Swami Rama, who reported of a demonstration given to him by his grandmaster:

> My grandmaster said, "I am going to give you wisdom. I am going to demonstrate for you." He said he could leave his body and enter someone else's body and then come back to his own body again. He said he could change his body at will. The thought flashed in my mind, "He wants to cast off his body and wants me to immerse it or bury it," but suddenly he said, "It's not that." He was replying to my thoughts. He instructed me to go inside the cave and again check if there was any outlet or hidden door, but I had already lived in that small cave for more than a month, and I thought there was no point in checking the cave again. I did as he ordered, and as I had seen before, it was a small rock cave with only one entrance having a wooden portico outside. I came out and sat under the portico with the lama next to me. He told us to come nearer to him and hold a wooden plate which was like a round tea tray. When we held the tray, he said, "Do you see me?"
>
> We said, "Yes."
>
> In my ignorance I said, "Please don't try to hypnotize me. I won't look at your eyes."
>
> He said, "I am not hypnotizing you."
>
> His body started becoming hazy and that haziness was a human form like a cloud. That hazy cloud human form started

moving toward us. Soon in a few second's time, the cloud disappeared. We found that the plate which we were holding started becoming heavier. After a few minutes, the wooden plate again became light as it was before. For ten minutes the lama and I remained standing holding that plate and finally sat down waiting in great suspense and awe for something to happen. After ten or fifteen minutes, the voice of my grandmaster told me to get up and to hold that wooden plate again. When we held the plate, it started becoming heavier and again the cloudy form reappeared in front of us. From the cloudy form, he came back to his visible body. This amazing and unbelievable experience was a confirmation. He demonstrated this *kriya* once again in a similar manner. Perhaps that day will never come when I can speak about this to the world. I would like to do so, because I feel that the world should know that such sages exist and that the researchers should start researching such secret signs. Miracles like this show that a human being has such abilities and in the third chapter of the Yoga Sutras, Patanjali, the codifier of yoga science, explains all the *siddhis*. I do not profess or claim that such *siddhis* are essential for self-enlightenment, but I want to say that human potentials are immense, and as the physical scientists are exploring the external world, the genuine yogis should not stop exploring the inner abilities and potentials.[2]

To understand how and why bilocation is possible we must first admit that bilocation always happens only to deeply spiritual people – saints, founders of religions, and spiritual masters who have spent years in intense spiritual practice. To understand how it is possible, we have to turn to what these individuals say about it, and to the spiritual teachings from traditions that recognize the phenomenon.

The explanation starts with death.

Most religions teach that we have an immortal soul that survives after death. Many people believe that when they die, their spirit leaves the physical body. This is true. Thousands of near-death experiences confirm this, and we also have the confirming teachings of religion founders or

---

[2] *Living with the Himalayan Masters*, Swami Rama (Himalayan International Institute of Yoga Science and Philosophy of the U.S.A., Honesdale: PA, 1986), p. 424-426.

saints themselves. People who "died" during surgery or accidents often report floating above their bodies, watching everything that happened – including the frantic efforts to revive them.

In nearly all these accounts, the same thing happens: an individual's spirit separates from their physical body and takes on an ethereal form of subtle matter like pure energy. The individuals often see their own body lying below them, lifeless and still as they remain existent in this spiritual body.

This separation of spirit from body suggests that our spirit can exist independently of the physical form. If this separation can happen at death or near-death, it raises the possibility that a highly trained or spiritually advanced individual could, under certain conditions, consciously separate their spirit from their body while still alive. Those who can do so achieve this success through spiritual practice.

Bilocation, then, would not simply be an illusion or hallucination, but a real projection of the spirit into a second location while the physical body remains elsewhere. The spirit, being freed – or partially freed – from physical constraints through spiritual practice, could appear elsewhere either visibly, invisibly, or sometimes only to certain observers.

This would explain many historical accounts of saints and spiritual leaders appearing in two places at once: praying in a monastery while simultaneously aiding someone in distress miles away, but it doesn't yet explain how the spirit condenses into tangible form. In most traditions that record bilocation – Christianity, Judaism, Islam, Buddhism, Hinduism, Taoism and others – the common factor is intense spiritual refinement of the concerned individual combined with a life dedicated to service, humility, and devotion. Thus, bilocation seems to arise as a byproduct of deep spiritual evolution, where the spirit, no longer tightly tethered to the physical body, acts with a freedom that most people never experience.

Most religions share an underlying basic idea that we possess an immortal spirit, our spirit is trapped within our physical body during life, and is set free at death. When we die – or during near-death experiences – our spirit leaves the physical body, a process often described as being like shedding a material body shell, sheath or husk that it once permeated to serve as the animating force of the physical form. The inner spiritual self, or soul, was the reason that the physical matter of a body could exhibit both life and consciousness in the first place. Life and consciousness are not just the product of biochemical-electrical process but require the presence of a higher subtle life force energy as well.

Many spiritual traditions teach that if a person dedicates themselves to the right kind of spiritual practice for long enough, the connection between the physical body and the spirit weakens, allowing the spirit to leave the body at will without causing death. Spiritual disciplines such as deep prayer, meditation, fasting, asceticism, breathing practices and specific yogic or mystical practices are said to purify the inner subtle body and gradually weaken its binding to our physical form. Over time, this is certainly what has allowed advanced practitioners – saints, sages, mystics – to free their inner spirit and project it across distances.

This creates two bodies: the physical body and a spiritual body, often called the astral, etheric, deva, or subtle body. Eastern religions often describe this spiritual body as being made of our vital energy, known as Qi or Prana.

However, in those same religions the idea gets more complex. Traditions with advanced spiritual teachings, like Hinduism, Yoga, Taoism, Buddhism, Sikhism, and others, state we actually have *five* potential spiritual bodies, with the physical body being just the first.

These teachings explain that if someone, now centered in their subtle spirit body rather than the physical body, continues deep spiritual practice, a higher spiritual body can emerge out of the subtle astral body that seems to be the new center of their self. In other words, it's not just that our physical body surrounds our spirit or soul – it's that our inner subtle body itself wraps an even higher spiritual self that is more truly the "real us." Through continued spiritual effort, this higher spiritual self can be released just as an astral subtle body was released from the physical body.

To put it another way, it is not just that matter wraps our subtle body, which is composed of the life force (vital energy) animating our physical body, but that our inner subtle body that serves as our life force, and which ultimately powers our consciousness, encases an even higher version of our spirit that is released if that astral spiritual self continues an ardent degree of spiritual cultivation.

As stated, *many* spiritual traditions teach that we have five possible bodies, not just one. You will be surprised to see how many! Spiritual ascension – no matter which religion you follow – follows the same pattern: through deep, consistent spiritual practice, you cleanse your inner nature and gradually weaken the connection between your true self (your spirit) and the *non-essential material layers that are not the true you*. You "shed," "burn away," "extinguish," "negate" or "break free" from these lower coverings, which are like the disposable husks that wrap a cob of golden corn, in order to reveal a higher spiritual self that is closer to being the ultimate perfected self that you truly are. You must engage in spiritual practices and work to purify your thinking, energy and behavior in order to climb this ladder of ascension.

In short, true spiritual practice strips away the lower physical and mental layers attached to you. Through devotion to spiritual (religious) practices you purify yourself by removing everything that does not reflect your highest nature. Hinduism says that you free your *atman* – your true, divine, highest core self – from the impurities of lower natures that defile its purest state of existence and thereby hide its perfection due to those pollutions.

One unstated goal of religion and spiritual practice is to get started at this ladder of ascension by generating an independent astral body – a subtle body of pure life force, or Prana – without having to die to experience it. This requires intense training along a *regular systematic schedule of spiritual practices* that transform your body, mind, behavior and inner energy to higher levels of purity.

As you practice, the subtle energies permeating your body slowly separate themselves from their lower octaves, or degrees of impurity. A new, higher-energy body eventually escapes from being bound to the matter of your physical nature, still connected to your old body but now able to move freely, like a hand that can slip in and out of a glove. This new subtle body can leave the physical body at will, freeing you from the limits of material physical existence – while still using your old body when needed.

This is a simplified explanation of the process behind the accomplishment of bilocation without going into the details behind this phenomenon of materialization. Before we proceed any further in explaining the details, let us first prove this basic claim of five bodies since the explanation depends upon this common doctrine of many religions.

These higher bodies aren't automatic. They are only accessible through dedicated spiritual cultivation practices. At death, everyone naturally sheds the physical body and rises in a subtle energy body within the earthly heavenly plane. But without ongoing spiritual practice, the journey stops there. Depending on one's virtue and effort at spiritual work, after the subtle body dies, the spirit can either reincarnate in the human world again, be reborn to heavenly subtle-bodied parents, or ascend into a higher Causal body due to fervent spiritual practice while a deva. These are the common spiritual teachings of the traditions which recognize the five bodies.

HINDUISM

The Hindu sage **Sri Siddharameshwar Maharaj** (1888-1936) of the Inchagiri Sampradaya, taught that we possess five potential bodies: the Physical, Subtle, Causal, Supra-Causal (Cosmic), and Paramatman body. The Supra-Causal body, also called the Great-Causal or Mahakarana body, corresponds to the Turya state of Vedanta.

Sadguru Sadafal Deoji Maharaj (1888-1954) of the Vihangham Yoga tradition – a Nath Siddha lineage – taught a similar structure: from the Gross Physical body, we ascend to the Subtle body, and can further ascend to achieve a Causal body, Prime Causal body, and finally a Superconsciousness body. These are known technically as the *Sthula deha, Sukshma deha, Karana deha, Mahakaran deha,* and *Hansa deha* in the Nath tradition.

The Tamil saint **Ramalinga Swamigal** (1823-1874), also known as "Vallalar," described a similar progression: from the unripe Physical body we can cultivate a purified Prana body (the subtle body of the devas in the earthly heavenly plane located surrounding us), body of Vibrations (the Causal body), a Wisdom-Light (Supra-Causal) body, and finally a Body of Immanence (a Superconsciousness body). He wrote that through the "fire of yoga" (a collection of intense spiritual practices) *the physical body of impure elements was slowly transformed into a body of pure elements.* This explains the gradual attainment of the subtle body through the yogic road of spiritual practices.

The *Taittiriya Upanishad* and the great sage **Adi Shankara** (c. 788-820 BC or 686-718 BC) of Advaita Vedanta both teach that our True Self is hidden beneath five coverings, wrappings or sheaths (*koshas*), much like layers of an onion except for the fact that these sheaths interpenetrate one another. Buddhism calls them *skandhas* (aggregates), and Sufism calls them *veils*. Rabbi Isaac Luria simply called them "layers" while Padre Pio called them parts of his personality.

In Kashmir Shaivism, these five *kosha* coverings are echoed in the concept of *kalas* – planes or worlds representing the stages that pure consciousness undergoes descending into matter, which is a concept shared by Sufism. Similarly, the sage **Gorakhnath** (11th century) describes five phases of the Divine Shakti's self-manifestation, each one giving rise to a distinct realm of existence and thus a new spiritual sheath. These five bodies allow the soul to experience five different realms of existence, each with its own level of freedom and power.

The five sheaths (or bodies) are not mere metaphors – they are actual layers of condensed energy from higher planes that become compressed or aggregated as matter within our level of human existence. They encase our highest self in a series of bodies that interpenetrate one another completely since they correspond to different energy planes or fields of existence.

The five *koshas* of Adi Shankara, which are fundamental tenets of Advaita Vedanta, are:

- ***Annamaya kosha***: the physical "food" body composed of gross matter
- ***Pranamaya kosha***: the energy body composed of Prana (life force)
- ***Manomaya kosha***: the mind body of thought processes
- ***Vijnanamaya kosha***: the wisdom and knowledge sheath of inner knowing
- ***Anandamaya kosha***: the innermost layer known as the bliss sheath

These layers intertwine but can be separated through spiritual practices. Your true *atman* – your eternal self that is your real self at the core of all these sheaths – is covered by these layers, but by spiritual effort you can systematically peel these sheaths away as independent bodies that remain on different heavenly realms of existence to eventually reveal your naked, truest self.

The *Taittiriya Upanishad* (2.2) explains: "*The self made of food (annamaya) is indeed the physical form. Within it is the self made of Prana (pranamaya), which is subtler and fills the former.*" In other words, your life-force body made of subtle energy resides inside your physical body, permeating it through interpenetration, and deeper still are higher energy bodies interpenetrating the lower bodies waiting to become differentiated so that they can emerge.

The first sheath or body that we have is the *annamaya kosha* (foodstuff body), which is our physical body. This is the material physical body that you are using right now, but inside it is a subtle body that is giving it life energy and its consciousness. So, ascending upwards from our physical body to higher spiritual realms in progressive sequence, next there is a *pranayama kosha* (subtle body made of Prana, or Qi), *manomaya kosha* (Causal body made of Shen), *vijnanamaya kosha* (Supra-Casual body) and *anandamaya kosha* (Superconsciousness or Immanence body).

These five *koshas* correspond to the five bodies of the spiritual path. Man's truest soul, which Hinduism calls the *atman*, is explained as being *covered* by these five *koshas* whereas you might more accurately say that the *koshas*, until they are unfurled from being aggregated with the human body, are *intermixed* as several different energy layers that can slowly become uniquely differentiated and then unraveled from one another so that they are released as separate bodies. Through spiritual practices you discard one body to arise in a higher body, but you remain connected to the lower body you just escaped from (until it dies) and still have control of its abilities as a type of appendage.

To put it another way, the sheaths described by Hindu masters, gurus or sages are different planes of energy condensed, compressed or agglomerated within the living matter of our physical body, but they can be gradually released through the processes of spiritual cultivation so that you can free yourself from a lower realm and arise as a more transcendent spiritual being who resides in a higher heavenly plane of existence, yet are still aware of the physical plane below.

Just as solid matter has more tenuous phases of existence (liquid, gas, plasma and so forth), the universe has different planes of existence that interpenetrate one another, and they are all agglomerated together in our dense plane of matter. However, through the practices of spiritual cultivation we can differentiate these energy realms from the human body and separate them out one-by-one because they have a distinctly different "purities," frequencies, vibrations or densities from one another. They are unique different existences where the lower realms cannot perceive the higher realms, but everything interpenetrates in the universe.

The *annamaya kosha* – which **Sri Nisargadatta Maharaj** (1897-1981) calls the "foodstuff body" – corresponds to our physical realm of matter that is condensed energy. You might colloquially say that matter is a condensing, compression, contraction, congealing or aggregation of higher energies such as Einstein proved possible in his famous energy-matter conversion equation. The fact that the subtle body (*pranamaya kosha*) is entrapped within the *annamaya kosha* has already been explained by the *Taittiriya Upanishad*, and so on this entrapment proceeds with the other *koshas* as well.

Spiritual cultivation – through yoga, meditation, devotion, breathing practices, mantra, *nei-gong* and virtue – works to *unbind* these energy layers from being entwined with your physical body. You then rise progressively into higher spiritual bodies, each freer and more powerful than the last, if you keep cultivating practices that purify your body's energy, your mind and your behavior. You repeat the same cultivation process of freeing yourself from whatever lower nature you possess at any level to arise in a new and higher spiritual body for as far as that process is possible, and Hinduism says there are five possible body attainments you can achieve.

Each new spiritual body retains a form recognizable as "you" but possesses vastly greater capabilities. The subtle body, for instance, is capable of the famous eight *siddhi* (miraculous powers) of yoga. The eight siddhis of *anima* (ability to shrink one's body), *mahima* (the ability to increase one's body size), *laghima* (the ability to become lighter), *garima* (the ability to become denser/heavier), *vasitva* (the ability to possess a human and take control over them), etcetera, for instance, are only the capabilities of the higher spiritual bodies and not a human body that learns yoga. Devas can lighten their bodies so that they can travel quickly, solidify their bodies enough to be able to rap on matter to make a sound in a room, and can shrink in size *(anima)* to enter into your brain that is the *siddhi* of *parakaya pravesanam* – the ability to enter the bodies of others that also includes a full body possession.

In the *Vimalakirti Sutra* of Buddhism, the 12-foot square room of Vimalakirti represents his brain, and all the great Buddhas, Bodhisattvas, spiritual masters and devas assemble inside it – by shrinking size using the power of *anima* – for a teaching session that is symbolized by the sutra. This is why people sometimes hear heavenly beings or even demons in their head, which we will explain in Chapter Four.

A new body once achieved also always resides on a different plane of existence (i.e. spiritual plane, sphere, *loka* or field) that interpenetrates with our own, but is invisible to our senses. The only way you can perceive such bodies is if you attain one yourself. Saints can see things in the higher metaphysical realms only because they attain bodies that reside on those planes of existence.

Let's summarize this information since it is new to most readers. According to Advaita Vedanta, we are composed of a *annamaya kosha* or gross physical body (*karya sharira*), a *pranamaya kosha* (inner subtle energy body made of Prana), *manomaya kosha* (mind-stuff sheath or Causal body), *vijnanamaya kosha* (wisdom sheath) and *anandamaya kosha* (bliss sheath). In Tantra Shastra, these five sheaths are the *paramjyoti, para, niskalasambhavi, ajapa* and *natrka* according to the *Jnanarnava*, which is a Jain text on meditation also known as *Yogapradipadhikara*, meaning "the Book that Illuminates Meditation." Most all schools of Hinduism recognize these five bodies, and they are found in other religions too.

Through intense spiritual practices that involve years of devotion – prayer, mantra, worship, pranayama, yoga, meditation, virtue cultivation (purity of behavior), *nei-gong* and so on – the inner spirit sufficiently purifies itself through spiritual practice as being distinctly different from the turbulent mixture of energies within our physical body, and finally bursts free from its physical shell, like a bird escaping out of a cage, and stands resplendent as an independent body made of Prana. A saint first achieves the emergence of his inner spirit as a subtle energy body, or deva body. Even though higher than one's physical body, this subtle body still carries within it the undifferentiated essences of yet higher bodies – the *manomaya, vijnanamaya,* and *anandamaya koshas* – waiting to be purified and liberated.

Think of it this way: Our next higher body, the subtle body, is an agglomeration of energies, from higher planes of existence, bundled together into a subtle form, which is also the case for our material body. Saints who master their practice can consciously free their inner spirit and arise in a more refined vehicle of existence – an astral body of prana energy, or even higher body depending upon how much progress they achieve in their spiritual cultivation.

This process repeats:

- The subtle astral body made of Prana eventually gives birth to a liberated *manomaya* sheath body

- The *manomaya* body made of Shen energy eventually generates the *vijnanamaya* body from within itself, after sufficient differentiation and purification
- And from there, the ultimate *anandamaya* sheath emerges after the *vijnanamaya* body achieves sufficient purification of its inner energies.

Ultimately, the bliss body (*anandamaya kosha*) remains – the vessel most closely aligned with pure consciousness. Some traditions equate it directly with the *atman*; others say the *atman* transcends even the bliss body. It this case it merges with the *Brahman* that Hinduism identifies as the absolute formless foundation of existence, or we simply say that our True Self is the formless, empty ground state of existence, and you realize this experientially when you attain the highest body existence possible To settle the imprecision because you still want to retain a consciousness that experiences bliss rather than annihilation, all that matters is that you continue spiritual practice to attain as high a body as you can go.

The point is, through disciplined spiritual practice, you don't just die and ascend. You *purify*, *evolve*, and *emerge* – ascending layer by layer or plane by plane – into higher bodies of energy, wisdom, and bliss, until you reclaim your full divine nature. This process is actualized through spiritual practices whereby you first free your *pranamaya kosha* (inner energy body made of Prana) from the shell of matter that encases it, and you thereby arise as a subtle energy-bodied spirit, which we colloquially call a "deva" or angel. You arise within a subtle spirit body that will still contain intermixed within itself the higher energies of the *manomaya*, *vijnanamaya* and *anandamaya koshas* (energies) until you attain the next higher spiritual body that splits off from the Prana energy body that you just arose within as your new center of manifest being.

To put it another way so that this becomes clear, an agglomeration of the *pranamaya*, *manomaya*, *vijanamaya* and *anandamaya koshas* constitute the subtle body or deva body, which is also sometimes called the astral body or etheric body. The way you attain this body is either through death or spiritual practices, which the saints actually accomplish and are then called "enlightened." By applying themselves to ardent spiritual practices for many years, a saint's inner spirit one day breaks apart from its physical shell and arises in a more transcendental body that is composed of Prana, an energy more subtle than matter. They free their subtle body inside them and arise as a deva.

The spiritual process of ascension always involves this sequence of arising in a higher spiritual body from the one you already possess, but the new body remains connected to your lower body (providing life force and consciousness) otherwise the old body would die. Hinduism simply says that you progressively strip your *atman* of its coverings or sheaths, arising in a new, more resplendent body vehicle each time you ascend. Buddhism calls this "birth through transformation."

When someone who has attained the subtle body composed of Prana next attains the *manomaya kosha* body, that Causal body will also contain within itself the energies of the higher *vijnanamaya* and *anandamaya koshas* until they can be defused from it after you generate the next higher body (*vijnanamaya* sheath) by purifying it out of the undifferentiated matrix of the *manomaya kosha* body.

The next higher spiritual body past the *manomaya kosha* will be composed of the *vijnanamaya kosha* together with the higher energies of the *anandamaya kosha* (and beyond) as a composite, while the achievement of the *anandamaya kosha* will stand independent by itself resplendent. Correction: the composition of the *anandamaya kosha* will contain *all* the remaining higher energy planes of the universe since they will still penetrate it with full permeation. They will serve as its life force and as the energies powering its consciousness. Those are the forces closest to the fundamental substratum of existence, and by achieving this stage you achieve "oneness" with the universe. You are always in a state of oneness with the universe, but at this stage you feel all the universal energies, recognize them, know them and can use this fact to perform deeds.

You can call the *anandamaya kosha* the *atman* because it is still a sentient living being with consciousness, so you can term it your highest physical self since it remains a manifested form. It is your highest self of *manifestation*.

Or, you can call all the remaining energies higher than it "pure consciousness" and identify them as your *atman* even though they are non-living energies (but they *are* the energies that power your consciousness). You can say these remaining higher energies are the foundation of life, or the foundation of consciousness, or your witness-consciousness, or you can say they are "primary consciousness" whereas they are always just pure energies, and it is the structure of your anatomy that allows consciousness to be born with such energies flowing through those structures.

Or, you can call your *atman* the singular Brahman empty ground state of the universe, in which case *atman* and Brahman are one ... but that's the case with every stage of manifestation anyway.

Hinduism says the *atman*, or true *manifested* self, is seamlessly united with Brahman. Depending upon which school of Hinduism you reference, you either equate your *atman* with your highest manifest self, your ultimate unmoving True Self that is the ultimate substratum of the universe (Brahman) where there is no such anything as manifestations or consciousness, or the remaining manifest energies above your final highest body attainment that would equate to the first energies of manifestation.

This short explanation of Hindu teachings demonstrates why various religions describe different heavens or spiritual realms – each one corresponds to a higher plane of existence that can only be accessed through spiritual bodies achieved through transformation made possible by spiritual practices of purification. To enter these realms, you must attain a higher spiritual body made of subtler, more refined energy that matches the purity of that plane of beingness. Without this transformation of ascension in a higher body, those realms remain out of reach. You wouldn't even know they existed because your sense organs could not access them. Later we'll discuss how this all generates the tangible body doubles of bilocation attributed to the saints.

The spiritual path, at its core, is about liberating your truest self – the very core of your immortal soul or *atman* – from the layers of energy (the *koshas*) that have become agglomerated with it over time. Essentially, the spiritual path of religious practice really means freeing your truest self-spirit of the *koshas* or energy shells still agglomerated with it by purifying them and then separating them out sequentially in turn. Shakyamuni Buddha described this in the *Surangama Sutra* by calling the *koshas* "*skandhas*" and explain that you progressively free yourself from them one by one.

These layers or wrappings are just sheaths of energy that have been condensed into the form of your body, but they can become unwrapped form one another to become separate look-alike bodies, though composed of higher substances. As you progress at doing this, you peel away these energetic shells to gradually reveal your pure, unbounded self.

You must pass through these stages of development one by one in sequence, like untying knots on a string one after another, to attain the ultimate goal of perfect sainthood and find your real ultimate self-nature, which is the foundational substance or essence that the entire universe came from. You can describe the progress in terms of body attainments (physical, subtle, Causal, Supra-Causal, Immanence), *koshas* or *skandhas*, heavenly realms or planes of existence, or via descriptions of the concomitant attendant consciousness that accompanies a relevant spiritual attainment. There are various ways to do it.

As explained, matter is really condensed energy that can be decomposed into various unique planes of existence quite different from one another, but science has not yet begun to understand this higher physics. Your highest self, or immortal *atman,* is wrapped in five layers of energy – each denser than the last. Through spiritual practice, you free yourself of these unnecessary shells and rise beyond them, ultimately existing in a purified, transcendental body untouched by lower vibrations. This journey of unwrapping the self from lower planes of being is the essence of real spiritual evolution.

DRUZE

In Druze (which is a Unitarian religion that combines aspects from Islam, Judaism, Christianity, Gnosticism, Neoplatonism, Pythagoreanism, and Hinduism) we have the five limits, which represent the five spheres of existence.

The Druze belief system includes a sophisticated understanding of reincarnation that relates to these planes of existence, with the top state being a reunification with the Cosmic Mind. In the Druze religion, reincarnation is seen as a path to spiritual purification, an opportunity for souls to achieve enlightenment, a state reached through knowledge and good deeds that opens the gates of paradise.

The sequence of successive progress along these lines corresponds to the five different bodies or shells mentioned in Hinduism.

First, we have the physical body of the **material plane**.

Next, there is the **Universal Soul sphere** where beings with a subtle body reside.

The subsequent **Logos (Word) sphere** represents the Mental Plane or realm of the Causal body.

The **Cause (Precedent) Sphere** relates to the Supra-Causal body.

The **Immanence sphere** corresponds to the Superconsciousness body stage of existence, also known as the Immanence body.

SIKHISM

In the Sikh tradition there are five stages of spiritual progress leading to the Ultimate Truth, or ultimate liberation. These stages are called Five *Khands* or *Panj Khands*, which means five regions or realms. The *Khands* delineate the different stages of spiritual ascent, and are outlined in the *Japji Sahib* (specifically in stanzas 34 to 37), the opening hymn of the *Guru Granth Sahib* composed by Guru Nanak Dev Ji.

The **Dharam Khand** or Realm of Righteous Action (Dutifulness) corresponds to the physical plane, and thus our physical body. Guru Nanak said, "The earth exists for dharma to be practiced." The word *dharam* has been employed in the sense of duty. Duty is usually performed either out of a sense of social responsibility or through moral awareness.

The **Gian Khand**, or Realm of Spiritual Knowledge, corresponds to the heavenly realm and thus the subtle body attainment that we experience upon death, or upon spiritual ascension. Devas who have subtle bodies finally receive true spiritual knowledge, which explains the name. As the spiritual aspirant moves forward, they enter Gian Khand, where the vastness of creation becomes clear. The soul begins to see the incredible order that governs the universe.

The **Saram Khand**, or Realm of Spiritual Efforts (Endeavors), corresponds to the next higher Casual body. The *Japji Sahib* says, "Forms of incomparable beauty are fashioned there." Here man strives against the last remnants of his ego which still afflict him in spite of his experiencing strong emotions of humility on this plane. Here the soul fashions itself into incomparable beauty that cannot be described; the consciousness, thinking and understanding are molded and purified to be like those of the gods and saints.

The **Karam Khand**, the Realm of Grace, corresponds to the Supra-Casual body, which is the next higher body. The process of liberation with grace initiated is now brought to completion. All sense of dualism ends. They do not die (do not reincarnate) and are no longer deceived by maya.

The **Sach Khand**, the Realm of Truth, corresponds to the Immanence or Superconsciousness body of full enlightenment or liberation. This is the highest level in this hierarchy where the individual attains a mystical union with God, the final state of the evolution of human consciousness. The *Japji Sahib* says, "In the realm of Truth, the Formless Lord abides."

In Sikh theology it is understood these stages are part of a spiritual journey which one must go through in life to unite oneself with their real soul. They involve a certain degree of "cleansing" and alignment of the mental emotion and physical planes which prepare the way for connecting with our soul. The delineation of the *Panj Khands* all starts with the term *pavarian*, i.e. rungs of a ladder, which denotes that they denote stages of mystical ascent.

JUDAISM

Rabbi Isaac Luria (1534-1572), the foundational figure of Lurianic Kabbalah, in his doctrine of *Partzufim* ("Divine Faces" or "Countenances") taught that the soul has multiple bodies or manifestations across multiple spiritual realms, and the "garment" of the body differs according to the realm it occupies.

In other words, man has five souls that reside on different planes of existence. These five realms and the bodies serving as garments (coverings or sheaths) for the soul are as follows:

- **Assiyah** (The World of Action): The physical body *(Guf)* operates here in the realm of purely material existence known as the World of Action, the World of Effects or the World of Making, which is the plane of matter.
- **Yetzirah** (The World of Formation): The astral body *(Ruach)* functions in this realm, which is related to the emotions and information that moves through the senses. This is the subtle realm above the realm of matter.
- **Beriah** (The World of Creation): The intellectual soul *(Neshamah)* is dominant here, the seat of the intellect. This level of the soul corresponds to the Causal body attainment.
- **Atzilut** (The World of Emanation): The higher soul *(Chayah)*, which means living essence, resides here (the Supra-Causal body) and is so etheric it has little connection with the body

but mostly dwells in the higher realms, connecting with the divine *Partzufim*.

- **Adam Kadmon** (Primordial Man): Nothing can be said about this soul level except that it represents the highest degree of awareness accessible to human beings, so this level is called primordial man, akin to the "manifest" *atman* of Hinduism. The *Yechidah* (singular essence) is rooted here, where the word "*Yechida*" roughly translates to "oneness" or "absolute" unity. Hence, this is the spiritual stage of attainment where one realizes their unity or oneness with all things because of their Superconsciousness body, its capabilities and that plane of existence.

According to Isaac Luria, one does not automatically have full access to these souls, but must work on themselves and merit to attain them. In other words, you must cultivate the path of spiritual practice, purity, virtue and merit provisioning. Unfortunately, a great many people spend their entire lives stuck in *nefesh*, living very materialistic and animalistic lives, never overcoming their desires and inclinations (*ruach*), nor achieving any kind of mental greatness (*neshamah*) so that they might transcend the lowest level of existence.

These soul levels are not separate universes, but reside one within the other through permeation. Although we give different names to the worlds, they are co-existent on top of one another. In the Lurianic plan, they are five intermediary agents in creation referred to as *Partzufim*. The spiritual body attainments each reside on one of these *Partzufim*, or realms of emanation/existence.

ISLAM

Meher Baba (1894-1969) explained the view of Sufism that there are five layers of a human being: the Gross body, Subtle body, Mental body, Universal body and Shiva-Atma or Paramatma body. In this Islamic framework, the *bhautic sharir* is the gross physical body, the *adhyatmic sharir* is the subtle energy body, and the *mansik sharir* is the mental or Causal body.

In some Sufi schools, the creation of the universe with all its energies and forms is seen as a Divine Descent that creates five realms of manifestation through a gradual emanation from the Absolute. Sometimes Sufism terms the universe an "effusion" of the Divine because the manifest cosmos is composed of energy layers. At the top of this chain is **Allah**, the unmanifest, formless, singular uncreated origin of all things. Allah just means the Primordial level of all existence, the fundamental substratum of all things that is not a living being.

This primordial reality, which is an utterly pure ground state that has no attributes or qualities, is therefore beyond all conception. You cannot make an image of It. Allah is the primordial level of Creation before there is anything we can call Creation, so Buddhists say that it is "empty" of all phenomena. In Hinduism, Allah is known as **Parabrahman**, **Nirguna Brahman**, **Purusha** or **Brahman** depending upon which school of Hinduism you reference.

For Sufism, the formless origin or ground state substratum is also called **Alam-i-HaHoot**, the Realm of "He-ness" or pure Is-ness where there is nothing other than itself. It is Absolute Alonehood (*Ahdiyat*) – unmanifest, unknowable, and beyond thought or imagery since it has no qualities. Aloneness means without phenomena or attributes, hence *Alam-i-HaHoot* is "The Unknowable and Incomparable Realm." Islam's prohibition against depicting Allah reflects this truth: Allah cannot be imagined because Allah is beyond form, attributes, qualities, characteristics or phenomena. The closest conception you can make of it is to think of it as infinite empty space that is empty of everything. Thus it is pure, unchanging, eternal.

From this pure ground state, the first manifestation emerges: **Alam-i-YaHoot**, the Realm of First Manifestation whose existence depends upon its substrate, Allah. Though distinct in appearance, manifestation is not separate from Allah as an independent entity. *Alam-i-YaHoot* (the first manifestation) is by definition an attribute or quality of the foundational ground state – Allah – and this first stage of divine descent is called the "Light of Muhammad."

This is the realm of *Wahid-ul-Wujud* – Absolute Unity, a singular Unitary Existence that encompasses everything infinitely. It is the very first step, or emanation, of creation, and thus in Hinduism it corresponds to **Ishvara** or **Saguna Brahman** since these are the first realms, phases, planes, stages or steps of manifestation from which all else is derived. This is the ***dharmakaya*** or the **Tathagatagarbha** (womb of Buddhahood) in Buddhism. In Sufi teachings, this is the first attribute arising from the unmanifest Absolute.

In Sufi metaphysics, all things are made of God-substance. Though phenomena appear separate due to our mental perceptions, they are ultimately nothing but Allah, their primordial substance, essential nature, foundational material, substratum, or ground state. They may seem different or apart from Allah's undifferentiated formlessness (empty nature) but they cannot be other than Allah since everything is composed of Allah since everything comes out of Allah. This illusion of separate uniqueness stems from the workings of consciousness that spins an illusion of incorrect perception along with a lack of wisdom where we do not understand correctly.

In Sufi cosmology, the first emanation, **Alam-i-YaHoot** corresponds to the Superconsciousness body or *anandamaya kosha*.

The next level of manifestation is **Alam-i-LaHoot**, the Realm of Absolute Unity, where immanent divinity begins to manifest. It corresponds to the Supra-Causal body or *vijnanamaya kosha*. In Judaism this is the higher soul *Chayah*.

Then comes **Alam-i-Jabrut**, the Realm of Power, which aligns with the Causal Body and the stage of the Anagamin (the third-level Arhat level of Buddhism). This plane contains various levels of refinement and spiritual purity, so it can be divided into many grades of purification.

The next level of emanation is **Alam-e-Malakut**, the Realm of Souls. It is the domain of beings made of Prana (life energy), such as devas or subtle spirits. These beings have not yet reached the causal level and still reside in the plane of energy and form where they are often dominated by their emotions that have not yet been purified.

At the lowest level is **Alam-i-Nasut**, the Physical Realm – the world of matter where our gross bodies exist. Here, spiritual beings – while composed of all the higher energies – are encased in the densest layer of material forms. Through spiritual practice, we can shed these layers one by one, ascending to subtler realms and lighter bodies.

All of these realms exist simultaneously and interpenetrate one another. As we rise in higher spiritual bodies, we "extinguish" our attachment to the lower layers of existence or "negate" them – not by destroying them, but by transcending them, leaving behind densities unnecessary for our existence.

Sufi philosopher **Ibn Habash Suhrawardi** (1154-1191), through his esoteric doctrine of Illuminationism, used the metaphor of light to explain these five realms. The **Light of Lights** *(Nur al-Anwar)* is the unmanifest origin, pure radiance with no form – akin to **Nirguna Brahman, Allah** or the ***dharmakaya*** in Buddhism. At this absolute substratum stage of purity nothing manifests because it is a sole oneness, a singular substance or realm of absolute purity. From it, creation somehow unfolds like descending layers of dimming light – each of greater diminishing intensity than the last. In fact, Jewish mysticism similarly describes these layers of emanation as a "thickening of the light."

Meher Baba (1894-1969) also outlined the five ranks of spiritual attainment in Sufism, which corresponds to the five bodies:

1. **Rahrav** – the seeker or ordinary individual who has begun the spiritual path but has not yet attained any significant spiritual realization. This corresponds to the gross consciousness state of ordinary human experience, which Meher Baba calls "gross consciousness" that is entirely concerned with the gross physical world.
2. **Wali** – a friend of God, akin to a yogi who attains the subtle body achievement, and who can then can read anyone's mind anywhere in the world by entering into the brain.
3. **Pir/Sant** – a perfected yogi (spiritual teacher) who attains the Causal body.
4. **Sadguru/Mahayogi** – a "Perfect Master," one who reaches divine union (*Wasla*) by attaining the Supra-Causal body.
5. **Beyond-Beyond State** – an Avatar who represents the highest manifestation of God-consciousness, beyond even the Perfect Master state. Their supreme realization (*Wara-ul-Wara or Ghaib-ul-Ghaib*) is equivalent to the Paramatma state, or attainment of the Superconscious-Immanence body of Perfect and Complete Buddhahood, namely enlightenment.

These stages align closely with Hinduism's system of spiritual bodies, and with the fivefold scheme of other traditions. Most Christians are unfamiliar with these various ranking schemes, except for those familiar with the levels of spiritual accomplishment corresponding to the Great Schema in Orthodox Christianity.

When a Sufi saint displays miraculous powers, it is because they have awakened and embodied one or more of these higher spiritual bodies that has special powers within its own realm of existence that can produce effects that appear in our world of form.

BUDDHISM

In the *Diamond Sutra*, a foundational Buddhist text, Shakyamuni Buddha explains that enlightened beings possess five spiritual bodies, each capable of a deeper level of perception. He said that a fully enlightened being has a Human eye, Deva eye, Wisdom eye, Dharma eye and Buddha eye. These eyes are paired with the same five bodies we have been discussing – the Human body, Deva body (Subtle body), Mental body (Causal body), Dharma body (initial "*nirvana* with remainder" Supra-Causal body), and Buddha body ("*nirvana* without remainder" Superconsciousness body) – and represent advancing spiritual faculties of perception tied to different levels of being.

Furthermore, these five bodies parallel the five *koshas* in Hinduism and align with Buddhism's five **skandhas: form, sensation, conception, volition,** and **consciousness.**

In **Tantric Buddhism (Vajrayana),** the journey through these bodies is described as moving from:

- The **Physical Body,**
- To the **Impure Illusory Body** (subtle body),
- Next, the **Purified Illusory Body,**
- Followed by the **Clear Light Body** (or Dharma Body),
- And finally, the **Buddha Body** – the final stage of spiritual ascension or liberation, a perfected Enjoyment or Reward body of Complete and Perfect Enlightenment (a stage of No More Learning) made of very refined transcendental energy.

Buddhism also has another scheme for delineating the five bodies – the stages of Arhatship – which matches with those of the other religions previously cited. The individuals who achieve spiritual enlightenment (higher body attainments) in various religions – Arhats (Buddhism), Arahants (Jainism), Gurus (Hinduism), Saints (Christianity), prophets

(Judaism), etc. – are given different names but they achieve the same level of body-mind attainments *because this ladder of ascension is non-sectarian.*

The five stages of Arhatship are:

1. **Srotapanna** – the stream-enterer (an impure stage of the subtle body attainment, akin to asuras and the first *dhyana*)
2. **Sakadagamin** – the once-returner (a more purified stage of the subtle body, akin to devas and the second *dhyana*)
3. **Anagamin** – the non-returner (the Causal body attainment and the third *dhyana*)
4. **Arhat** – fully liberated (the Supra-Causal body attainment, or "*nirvana* with remainder" akin to the fourth *dhyana*)
5. **Great Golden Arhat** – a pinnacle stage of complete and perfect enlightenment or "*nirvana* without remainder" (the Immanence or Superconsciousness body attainment)

First, we have the human body.

Next, we have the subtle body, which is broken into two stages of Arhatship based on an individual's energetic (Prana) and ethical purity (virtuous behavior): the Srotapanna and Sakadagamin ranks of spiritual attainment.

The *Surangama Sutra* teaches that you attain the subtle body when your spirit breaks free from the physical body – the form *skandha*. Buddhism calls this initial liberation the **Srotapanna** stage, also known as the *"Joyous Ground Born of Separation,"* because finally escaping the physical shell brings great joy and happiness. This is the lowest stage of enlightenment, salvation, heavenly reward or liberation.

The next stage, **Sakadagamin**, represents a more refined subtle body achievement whose own Prana is more purified than the Srotapanna stage due to the fact the individual has engaged in lots of spiritual practices and personal cultivation work, and thus their body and consciousness are more purified because the energy running through them is more refined. This level is called the *"Joyous Ground from the Production of Samadhi"* since at this stage, the vital energy that powers consciousness becomes more purified and your inner world – your mind – is therefore calmer and more focused than before. Accordingly, this mental realm is more pristine and stable than that of a Srotapanna Arhat, and one's mental realm is therefore called a

INCORRUPTIBLE BODIES AND BILOCATION MIRACLES

samadhi, or concentration.

Beyond the subtle body lies the Causal body corresponding to the **Anagamin** stage of Arhatship. This body exists on a higher energy plane than where the deva body resides. Causal-bodied beings live within the Realm of Form (*Rūpadhātu Loka*), which is above the Desire Realm (*Kāma Loka*) where devas reside. Beings in this higher realm all have bodies composed of more refined substances than those of devas, making them invisible to the devas. Just as we can't see devas, devas can't perceive these even higher beings since they live on a higher plane of purified existence.

Interestingly, those in higher realms *can* see into lower ones, and in some cases, influence or even control the thoughts and actions of those with "denser" bodies by entering into them and taking control over their minds. They can override someone's processes of consciousness with their body's mental energies because their own consciousness operates by using a more refined energy that is more foundational, and thus it can override the coarser energy levels of a lower realm.

Let's put it this way. You possess the ability of consciousness because your physical body is inhabited by a subtle body made of Prana, and it is this Prana energy that supplies the powers of your life and consciousness. Without this living energy you would be an inanimate substance, which is just another reason that AI - lacking a higher subtle body – is neither living nor truly sentient.

A deva body, on the other hand, is filled by a Causal body whose energies have not yet become sufficiently differentiated and purified for it to become liberated from its subtle body shell. The more refined, higher energies of a Causal-bodied being – called "Shen" in Taoism – can enter into a deva or human and override their consciousness with thoughts and emotions. Those energies are of the same nature as the ones that power consciousness for devas, yet more foundational because of their refinement, so they are higher and can override the minds of beings below. A super-Causal body is composed of even higher energies – called "Later Heavenly Energy" in Taoism – so it can override the consciousness of humans, devas (subtle bodied beings) and Causal-bodied beings, and so on it goes.

Buddhism refers to the Causal body or Anagamin stage of Arhats as the *"Wonderful Blissful Ground of Separating from Joy,"* because while devas revel in joy and happiness, this joy is seen as a coarse mental disturbance to the calmer level of consciousness experienced by Anagamins. To the Causal-bodied mind, the mental factor of bliss becomes calmer, steadier, and serene because the energy is far more refined than that experienced by the subtle body. This stability comes from the purer, more refined energy powering consciousness and one's life force at this stage.

The Causal body is of such high purity that Anagamin Arhats can perform some miraculous feats – restoring sight to the blind, stopping trains, and levitation.

Going even higher is the Supra-Causal body, attained by full **Arhats**, whose miraculous powers are even greater. This body resides in the "formless realm" (*Arūpadhātu Loka*) and is nearly pure energy – capable of incredible shape-shifting and extraordinary subtlety. It corresponds to the volition *skandha* in Buddhism and the *vijnanamaya kosha* in Hinduism. This body-mind attainment is known as *"nirvana with remainder"* – meaning that one final body still remains to be attained before complete enlightenment.

Buddhism calls this attainment the *"Ground of Clear Purity from Casting Away Thought,"* which reflects the deep clarity and absence of distractions to concentration experienced by those with this body. Consciousness at this level flows so smoothly and purely – because the energy that powers consciousness is so refined and smooth compared to the lower levels of existence – that the practitioner enjoys unmatched concentration, inner silence, unwavering peace and focus.

When you attain the **Supra-Causal body** by refining the energies of the Causal body through spiritual practices, you gain a form that doesn't decay like ordinary bodies. It's made of long-lived, essences – often called "light" rather than matter although it is not composed of photons. This long life is why such beings are said to be immortal, no longer bound to the lower realms of reincarnation. This transcendental body doesn't need to interact with denser energies anymore, so it is completely free of matter, and the fact that it can no longer get stuck to them allows you to escape the cycle of birth and death in the lower physical worlds forever.

Even if someone at this stage must die, they retain life memories that can carry into a future incarnation – something seen in some lower-level Arhats too. This Supra-Causal body can also create (split off) energy copies of itself that can be sent across the world to perform separate missions such as give people thoughts, energy or even to perform small tasks. If a saint talks to someone who has a different language than his own, and uses a *nirmanakaya* to overlap their body, the individual will then be able to understand whatever the saint is saying despite the difference in languages. This has been seen in the case of many modern Greek Orthodox saints, and even with Padre Pio.

The Supra-Causal body also has the ability to condense its energy to form a tangible body we can see and touch, and its *nirmanakaya* emanations (after training) have this power too. This is what is responsible for bilocation, which is either a *nirmanakaya* projection body or the Supra-Casual body itself ... or it is the Superconsciousness body or one of its *nirmanakaya* emanations. Lower-level Arhats – physical, subtle or Causal bodied beings – cannot create body doubles or perform bilocation by condensing their body into a tangible materialization. This is only possible for individuals who achieve the Supra-Causal body or higher.

In Buddhism, this body is known by many names: the **Clear Light Body, Wisdom Body, Jnana Deha, Dharma Body, Rainbow Body**, or **Arhat Body**. It is said to be "one with the universal life," because its refined energy permeates all the lower realms and can thus sense what happens to any living being in those realms should the individual choose. That is why someone can pray or mantra to a saint (with this body or higher) and they can hear their call to respond. This unity with lower life allows it to witness the universe, perceive the minds of lower beings, and access their knowledge and wisdom effortlessly. Thoughts and emotions made of coarser energies are easily "read" by this more refined consciousness, which is why saints are said to be able to read people's minds or "know their hearts."

When someone attains this stage, we say that "their inner wisdom opens" – hence it is called the **Wisdom Body**. They no longer need to physically access a brain to read thoughts because they can sense the energy of thought patterns directly in the environment and learn this way. Using *nirmanakaya* emanations – energy projections or "body doubles" – they can enter other beings, including intelligent animals like elephants, horses, parrots, and dogs, and retrieve memories stored in neurons as well as understand or influence their consciousness.

The capabilities of the Supra-Causal body, or even just the Causal body, put the modern transhumanist movement to shame. In fact, transhumanism has gone off track by emphasizing technology to achieve specific goals instead of personal spiritual development that achieves far, far more than it has imagined. In one sutra, Shakyamuni Buddha even said that if he explained all the things that the highest bodies can do you would simply not believe him, so transhumanism has been putting its energies in the wrong direction that is actually harmful to human evolution and your afterlife states. What transhumanists should be pursuing are the higher transcendental spiritual bodies with their "greater than human" capabilities including access to higher realms of perfection that scientists might call dimensions. These spiritual bodies, which virtuous people who have purified their conduct can achieve through the road of spiritual cultivation,[3] are capable of far more than transhumanists can ever hope to achieve through the avenue of technology augmentation and its other pathways of emphasis.

The masters who attain the Supra-Causal body can also perceive the etheric record of time – the past and future pattern of events, also known as the akashic record. This ability gives rise to prophecy of what is to come and other profound insights, which is why many traditions associate this level with supreme wisdom. It is also capable of far more superpowers than can be listed.

As stated, the Supra-Causal body can generate (split off) or "project" copies of itself – called *nirmanakaya* bodies, emanation bodes or projection bodies – that are made of its same energies. These can appear in the world as invisible helpers or even take physical form (because they can condense their energy into tangibility), perform specific deeds, and vanish again. An Arhat or Great Golden Arhat can even generate a *nirmanakaya* that looks like someone else so that it can materialize in the subtle realm to welcome someone into the afterlife, while also beaming to them emotions of peace, love, acceptance and welcome. As a general rule, the older the sage the greater their *nirmanakaya* projection skills, and some older spiritual masters can generate hundreds to thousands of *nirmanakaya* every moment to address the prayers of people with helpful thoughts or inspiration.

When a saint appears in a distant location with a body double it can be because their Supra-Causal body itself (not a *nirmanakaya* projection) condenses its energy to manifest there while their physical form remains

---

[3] See *The Inner Secret Teachings of Daoism* for methods of *simultaneously* practicing different inner energy purification techniques, which is key, where each type is based upon different Qi purification principles, thus speeding one's progress since the pathway is no longer hidden.

elsewhere, and at others time the foreign appearance is a *nirmanakaya* projection that materializes into a tangible form, which the military calls particle-ization.

A Supra-Causal body has great control over its own internal energies, which it can move around in all sorts of patterns. This body can also move internal energies in others because its energy is more foundational than the energy composing lower-bodied beings. If a Supra-Causal body or one of its *nirmanakaya* enters you, it can trigger sensations like kundalini movements, inner heat or cold, and various types of vibrations. Often, when people feel strong inner energy during prayer or meditation – what Christians might call the "Holy Spirit" – it's actually the result of some spiritual master's *nirmanakaya* projection working within them to help purify their subtle body. These energy currents purify your Prana through friction that cleanses it over time, thus preparing you to attain the independent subtle body achievement. To become a saint you must undergo many years of this frictional process and suffer all sorts of internal energy sensations, including feelings of great heat and cold or sometimes even pain, often accompanied by intense emotions and wild inner energy movements.

Beyond the Arhat stage lies the ultimate state: the **Great Golden Arhat**, known in Hinduism as the attainment of the **Immanence body** or **Superconsciousness body**. This is the stage of Complete and Perfect Enlightenment, or the Stage of No More Learning (No More Training or Non-Practice) that is called "*nirvana* without remainder" in Buddhism. At this level, there is no higher spiritual body to attain. The soul – the *atman* – reaches its highest body potential and a penetrating unity with the energies of the universe while still retaining a conscious form.

This final body is associated with the consciousness *skandha* in Buddhism, the *anandamaya kosha* (bliss sheath) in Hinduism, and countless names from the other religions we have previously mentioned. It is also known as the **Tathāgata body** – the perfected body of Buddhahood. It is also the tenth *bhumi* of the Bodhisattva path, which represents the highest realization possible.

This is the highest or purest stage of the *atman* in Hinduism within the hierarchy of manifest bodily sheath attainments. In other traditions, this ultimate state is known by other names: the *insān al-kāmil* or "Perfect Human" in Islam, the "true man" or "real man" in Taoism, "God Consciousness" in Kashmir Shaivism, the "*tzadik*" in Judaism, and *nirvikalpa samadhi* in Hinduism. It is a body composed of energies belonging to the highest transcendental energy plane we can reach while still maintaining a body.

As you progress through these stages, your consciousness becomes more pristine or purified. Each new body means that the energy that powers its life force and mind is at a higher stage than that body, so that energy is more refined that the body matrix containing it. That being the case, with each new body the vital energy (life force) that powers the mind and life is more refined. Each upgrade to a higher body therefore brings greater clarity, stability, and purity of awareness. To put it differently, at every level your mind is powered by the energy of the next higher realm, until it reaches this final stage of full enlightenment.

At this highest possible body attainment equivalent to full enlightenment, you realize your unity with all things in the universe through interpenetration or entanglement, which is called the Flower Ornament (*Avatamsaka Sutra*) view in Buddhism, and you realize that the ultimate source nature of the universe permeates all things as their unmoving essence.

In Buddhism, the foundational pure, eternal, unchanging essence of the universe (which is absent, devoid or empty of phenomena since they have not come into being) is called the *dharmakaya*, and so various religions in the world that share this same idea teach people to practice "*dharmakaya* meditation" by putting their mind in tune with its nature, i.e. empty of thoughts while maintaining alertness or awareness instead of no-thought sleep. This is "emptiness" or "empty mind" meditation. Thus, this is also often called "clear light" meditation (since awareness still shines), "empty space" meditation, "no-thought" meditation, "presence" or just "pristine awareness" (that is detached from thoughts). There are lots of similes for this basic style of meditation practice. Even Christianity, Islam and Judaism practice this way.

Your consciousness, at the stage of the Great Golden Arhat attainment, is powered by whatever energy realms are yet higher that cannot be turned into a physical being. However, to simplify teachings, the spiritual schools of the East simply say that you realize that your genuine True Self, or *atman*, is the ground state original essence beyond your highest form body and beyond all those manifesting energies. Your real *atman* is the pure, unchanging ground state or fundamental essence of All Reality that birthed the manifest universe. It is everywhere, in all things. Your highest manifest *atman*, *jiva* or self, however, is the highest body attainment you can reach.

This is why many of the saints and spiritual masters in Chapter One explained bilocation by referring to the singular empty primordial essence that gave birth to the universe of endless forms, which is an analogy for their ability to sit motionless in one place and generate multiple *nirmanakaya* just as the unmoving central ground state of existence generates a multitude of forms. The empty primordial essence, the ground state of all existence absent of forms that is everywhere, has generated a universe that is a multiplicity of forms. When a saint or sage attains the Superconsciousness or Immanence body, they realize their intrinsic oneness with the empty original essence that composes them and can say, "I, too, can generate myriads of forms (bodies) everywhere."

Hence, we saw many saints verifying all we have discussed by basically proclaiming, in response to their bilocation, "I have achieved the Superconsciousness body, the stage of the Great Golden Arhat that is one with the empty original nature that has generated all forms, and so I too can generate multiple bodies." They were basically just indicating that they had achieved the highest transcendental body achievement. For instance,

> Neem Karoli Baba said: "I sit in one place, but my *lila* (divine play) is everywhere."
> Ramana Maharshi said, "Where am I not? The Self is everywhere."
> Swaminarayan said: "Does the sun not shine everywhere at once?"
> Ramakrishna said, "The body is like a lamp. The flame can be seen in many mirrors at once."
> Rabbi Isaac Luria said: "The soul of a *tzaddik* (righteous man) can be in many places at once."
> Baal Shem Tov said: "The light of Shabbat is infinite – can one man not share it in many places?"
> Shams Tabrizi said: "The body is a shadow. The sun (Shams) can cast its light wherever it wishes."
> Lahiri Mahasaya said, "The body is a mere shadow of the soul. The soul can be wherever it wishes."
> Lu Dongbin wrote in *The Secret of the Golden Flower*: "The sage is like the moon – one in essence, but reflected in ten thousand waters."

Zhang Sanfeng wrote a poem: "Above the peaks, one body; In the valleys, ten thousand shadows."

CONFUCIANISM

Most people are unaware that **Confucianism**, particularly in the teachings of **Mencius** (372 BC – 289 BC), also outlines stages of spiritual cultivation that correspond to the five transcendental bodies.

Mencius called the subtle body achievement – equivalent to the Srotapanna Arhat – the stage of **"Faith"** or **"Belief."** This is because, upon reaching this level, you gain access to the astral heavens and can interact with the deva spiritual being residents. Therefore, you develop *trust, confidence, faith and belief* in the spiritual path you've been following to get you there even though there may have been people throughout your life who criticized you for taking religious practices and self-improvement so seriously.

All the heavenly beings around you know that the spiritual pathway involves spiritual cultivation practice, everyone can see demonstrations of the higher transcendental bodies by enlightened spiritual masters, and even meet beings from other world systems doing similar types of cultivation according to their cultures. Thus, Mencius called this the stage of Belief or Faith because you gain confidence in the spiritual practices you must perform going forward.

The subsequent stage of spiritual progress in Confucianism is called **"Beauty."** This corresponds to the Sakadagamin stage and involves further purification of the subtle body of Prana to develop a higher degree of purified energy. Technically speaking, at this stage you are really purifying your Prana and Shen energy since the next higher body, the Causal, will be born from the Shen energy that is the life force of the deva's Prana body. By refining your internal energies, you begin to "beautify" yourself – your Prana becomes cleaner, more luminous, and more aligned with the purity of virtuous behavior.

All astral or deva bodies – whether they belong to naturally born devas, successful spiritual practitioners, or deceased humans – are composed of Prana, but vary in refinement, namely the purity of their Prana. This variation gives rise to two different levels of classification. In Buddhism, these correspond to the first and second dhyana levels; 1st-2nd and 3rd-4th Bodhisattva *bhumis* (stages of enlightenment); and the lowest Arhat stages of the Srotapanna and Sakadagamin attainments. In Hinduism, these two levels are signified by the *vitarka* and *vicara samadhi* states.

In broader spiritual typologies, the degree of one's virtuous behavior is usually used as a proxy for Prana purity that distinguishes subtle-bodied beings into asuras and devas; bad goods and guys, or people who haven't worked too hard at freeing themselves from their carnal nature and materiality, and those who have.

Mencius referred to this phase of spiritual work as **"extending and fulfilling"** – meaning that once attaining the subtle body as a deva you must now continue cultivating and refining that body to the point where a new, higher body-mind complex can emerge from it: the Causal body composed of an energy named Shen (Taoism) that is vibrationally more elevated, etheric or pure than Prana (Qi). The Causal body achievement marks the Anagamin stage of Arhatship.

This pursuit of Prana purification is exactly what is done in worldly religions through devotional worship, religious singing, prayer or mantra, charity work, meditation or quiet introspection, yoga, pranayama and other spiritual practices. While people recognize that purity of conduct is one of the sought after objectives, *most people don't know that Prana purification is the ultimate target of such practices.*

To summarize, you must first attain the deva body through your spiritual work. Now your spiritual task is to continue cultivating the purity of its inner energy, **"extending and fulfilling it,"** which is also called *beautifying it or perfecting it*. Once this purification reaches a certain threshold, you will generate a new and higher spiritual body out of its essence composed of a more refined energy than Prana. Just as your physical body gave rise to the Pranic subtle body, now the subtle body births the Causal body – a spiritual vehicle composed of a finer, more rarefied substance that Taoists call Shen.

This process is explained in **Vajrayana Buddhism**, which teaches that the **"impure illusory body"** (subtle body) can give rise to a **"purified illusory body,"** free from all gross matter and impurities – which is precisely this stage of transformation. It is also expressed in the Upanishadic concept of sheaths (*koshas*): the *pranamaya kosha* (energy body) contains the *manomaya kosha* (mind body), which simply needs to become liberated from the Pranic body after the *manomaya* energies are fully differentiated from being intermixed with Prana.

As Hinduism explains, the subtle body composed of Prana is filled by another self, made of Shen (*manomaya kosha*), the *manomaya kosha* is filled by the *vijnanamaya kosha* that resides within it, and the *vijnanamaya kosha* is filled by the *anandamaya kosha*. What emerges through the refinement of subtle energy is a higher spiritual energy that was previously bound within the matrix of the deva body. As spiritual cultivation proceeds, the inner Causal body's ties to the denser Pranic energies weaken, and the Shen energy differentiates itself to ultimately emerge as a new, independent body – the Causal body.

This process repeats for the generation of every new spiritual body. What interpenetrates throughout a deva's subtle body is the unrefined energy of a yet higher transcendental body that becomes differentiated from the deva's energy if that individual cultivates sufficiently. As the ties that bind the unpurified higher energies lessen due to becoming differentiated through purification, they eventually gain release because the binding thins. At that point of becoming so purified that it is different from Prana, it can finally separate from the shell of the subtle body. This happens after that individual cultivates a lot of spiritual practices to purify the vital energy of their subtle body, which takes approximately three years of devoted practice. This is why Tibetan masters typically go into secluded retreat for that amount of time. The accomplishment is basically the result of "beautifying" or purifying one's Prana and fulfilling the full potential of it.

Mencius next said that from the stage of Beauty as a base, "extending and fulfilling it until it shines forth is called great," which is calling the Anagamin attainment **"Greatness"** or **"Grandness."**

In **Nath Yoga**, this Causal body is referred to as the "body of vibrations" because it is made of a more refined substance than Prana that is free of the subtle body's heavier material nature, hence is easier to vibrate. The Causal body is tethered to the subtle body of Prana but composed of a more refined substance so it resides on a higher plane of existence. Every new spiritual body is more refined and thus more subtle than the previous one from which it emerged. These transcendental bodies remain invisible to lower planes but interpenetrate them completely as more foundational layers of reality. All the higher realms of energy interpenetrate the lower realms so it is just that a higher set of aggregates arises independently, once freed from the bindings of their shell, in a new independent body of their own.

Following this is the stage Mencius called **"Sagehood,"** which corresponds to the attainment of the Supra-Causal body – the body of a full Arhat. This vehicle transcends all lower energetic structures, including both Qi (Prana) and Shen materials, which is why it can sense vibrations or perturbations within all the lower realms of being that are denser fields of manifestation. Its abilities – often described as spiritual superpowers – are immense.

An Arhat is said to have achieved the fourth dhyana, which is the classical definition of enlightenment, so Mencius calls the Supra-Causal achievement becoming a **"sage."** This stage marks the birth of the *vijnanamaya-anandamaya kosha* complex, fully liberated from the shell of the Causal body that previously contained these essences. It is composed of a substance so pure that sages compare it to invisible or clear light that has become completely separated from matter. It belongs to a field where light and matter have become fully detached from each other in terms of relationships that might pull on each other.

Composed of an extremely refined energy – sometimes called Clear Light or Later Heavenly Energy – this body exists in a very high transcendental plane of existence that is closer in purity to the substance of the foundational essence. Taoists call it Later Heavenly Energy, which is the substance of the Supra-Causal body or Taoist stage of the "Celestial Immortal."

Like light splitting into many colors, the Supra-Causal body can separate off energy copies of itself called *nirmanakaya* emanations. These are like different wavelengths of light and can be projected to perform specific tasks – such as offering mental guidance, emotional healing, physical healing, inspiration, visions, dreams, or energy boosts to others. This is the primary mechanism by which saints and sages help people without their knowledge. When you pray to a saint for help, this is what usually provides assistance, if at all. When you pray to God for help, this level of being or the sage is usually the one who responds. Moreover, the *nirmanakaya* emanations of this level being can themselves cultivate and become refined enough to generate their own higher spiritual Superconsciousness bodies.

Consciousness at this stage, as with all stages of spiritual ascension, is still dependent upon the structure and processes of whatever body you have. The supernatural powers of each higher body don't manifest automatically; they must be trained and mastered. Each spiritual body is essentially a more purified replica of your prior self and thus still retains your previous ways of thinking until you change. If you don't evolve your ways of thinking, your perspectives and your habits or regular behaviors, these things may stay the same despite your physical ascension. As Guru Nanak said, the soul must fashion itself into incomparable beauty by molding and purifying its thinking, understanding and doing to be like those of the gods and saints. You must always grow by pursuing virtue, purity of conduct and shedding what is ignorant, non-compassionate, and flawed. True transformation requires not just energetic evolution but mental and psychological refinement at each stage.

Each higher spiritual body has greater capabilities and can accumulate more experiences than the body from which it arose. However, the memories of these higher bodies are not automatically imprinted into the lower ones unless the higher consciousness descends into and operates through the lower body – much like a snail retreating into its shell – and starts thinking about its higher memories so that those thoughts can then be embedded in the brain of the lower-level body. Basically, each spiritual body essentially lives a separate life independent from the others with its own awareness, memories, and focus.

For example, a spiritual master like **Pramukh Swami Maharaj** (1921-2016) of the Swaminarayan tradition, may appear to have an extraordinary memory for details – such as those involved in constructing temples or guiding disciples – but what appears as a superhuman memory is often the result of a higher spiritual body scanning or referencing the memories stored within his physical brain to recall details normally forgotten. A spiritual master or saint may momentarily retrieve that information, and this then makes them look like they have a super memory.

When a master is present in the physical world while his higher bodies are engaged elsewhere in higher realms, he may appear distant, distracted, "not present" or absent with a vacant look (the eyes look straight forward without there seeming to be anyone behind them), and from conversations people might describe them as seeming "empty." Only when those higher bodies return to rest within the physical shell does he appear more grounded, present and capable of wiser decisions than when he/she seems absent.

This ability to live in higher realms but return within the earthly shell to give teachings or advice explains why such individuals can preach detachment from worldly concerns – such as money, sex, power, difficulties and emotional entanglements. It is because the primary center of their identity no longer resides in the physical world, which is just seen as a world of play. The saint is operating on a different plane so the human-level factors don't matter because the human life-level has been negated as the center of his existence. However, within his highest realm he certainly faces the same issues we all do, so don't ever think that suffering disappears even though scriptures say so, nor believe that people are really as pure as they seem. Many are married upstairs but preach celibacy below, hence they certainly need money for their upper family. The hypocrisy in such preaching is simply a means to help guide people along a path of ascension where a master wants to place your full attention on spiritual work (and Prana purification) to advance upwards and escape the human realm.

As one continues ascending the spiritual path, a point is reached where the cultivation level becomes so advanced that it can no longer be measured or recognized by ordinary standards. In Confucianism, this stage is described as becoming **"Shen,"** or **divine** – the highest level of the Buddhist enlightenment *bhumis* in Mahayana Buddhism. This stage of Confucian "divineness" is equivalent to the Great Golden Arhat, Immanence Body, Superconsciousness body, and Buddha body or Tathagata stage of achievement. Like the Supra-Causal body, this highest of spiritual bodies can also generate *nirmanakaya* projections but they have the ability to themselves generate their own *nirmanakaya* projections! This is the highest stage of spiritual attainment.

TAOISM

According with these other spiritual traditions, Taoism also teaches that a human being possesses the latent potential for five progressively more refined bodies composed of distinctly different essences: Jing (the physical essence based on semen), Qi (Prana or life force energy), Shen (spirit), Later Heavenly Energy, and Primordial Heavenly Energy.

Taoism teaches that the stages of the spiritual path are achieved through exercises that purify the life energy of each spiritual body, in turn, as a new body is achieved, and these purifying transformations are achieved through *neijia*, *neidan* or *nei-gong* practice. The sequence of transformations is that "Jing transforms into Qi, Qi into Shen, Shen into Emptiness, and you have to abandon Emptiness to return to the Tao." Taoism calls each stage of attainment a "transmutation" achieved through "inner alchemy." For instance, it is not that Qi transforms into Shen but that out of your undifferentiated life force within your Qi body, refining that vital force through *neijia* spinning (and other) exercises will differentiate out the pure Shen energy. When the Shen body is differentiated out of the undifferentiated internal energy of the Prana body, Taoism calls this refinement or purification a transmutation.

In Taoism, spiritual cultivation can thus be divided into five steps:

Transforming grain (food) into Jing,
Transforming Jing into Qi *(Lian Jing Hua Qi)*,
Transforming Qi into Shen, or spirit *(Lian Qi Hua Shen)*,
Returning Shen to emptiness *(Lian Shen Huan Xu)*, and
Emptiness returns to the Tao *(Lian Xu He Dao)*.

A rough way to understand this Taoist progression is to begin with the body's physical sustenance. You eat grains and food to sustain your physical form, which was developed from the semen and ova of your parents – what Chinese internal alchemy calls **Jing**, which is the essential, inherited essence. This Jing-based body (our physical body) serves as the foundation for spiritual transformation.

The subsequent spiritual transformations of ascension that follow are:

- **Jing transforms into Qi**: When the physical body born of semen (Jing) is sufficiently purified and its essence conserved, the vital energy or Qi body (often equated with the subtle body or deva body made of Prana) can emerge. This is the subtle body composed of life force energy – what Hinduism calls the *pranamaya kosha*.
- **Qi transforms into Shen:** Through deeper cultivation, this Qi body is further refined into a more rarefied energetic structure known as the Shen body, equivalent to the Causal body or *manomaya kosha* in the Hindu schema, and corresponding to the Anagamin stage in Buddhism.
- **Shen transforms into Emptiness:** As the Shen body is purified, a new transformation occurs. The resulting Emptiness

body that is generated corresponds to the Supra-Causal body or Clear Light body of a fully enlightened Arhat – the attainment of a bodily structure devoid of any ties to the lower worlds as it abides in a realm transcending any material realms, which Buddhism thus terms formlessness. The fact that this body is denoted by invisible light and formlessness is why Taoism refers to this as Emptiness, although this term also designates this body's total break with the lower material realms.
- **Emptiness returns to the Tao:** The highest stage involves transcending even the Emptiness body devoid of matter attributes. Here, an even higher body is attained that is on par with the fundamental substratum layers of manifested Nature.

To restate this another way, Taoism says:

- When your Jing-based physical body undergoes sufficient purifying transformations, you generate a Qi body (a subtle deva body composed of Prana).
- When the Qi body is purified, you can generate out of it the Causal body composed of Shen energy.
- When the Shen body becomes purified, you can attain a stage called Emptiness, which corresponds to generating a Supra-Causal body, Dharma body, or Clear Light body in the Buddhist classification scheme. This is the stage of the Arhat, and the body is composed of Later Heavenly Energy (Qi).
- Finally, to complete the path, you must transcend even this highest form and generate the highest possible body vehicle, a Superconsciousness or Immanence body whose corresponding mental continuum is "considered" the Tao. This body is said to be composed of Primordial Heavenly Energy (Qi) and the rank of attainment is the Great Golden Arhat achievement.

Taoism even has names for these levels of achievement. It explains that if you work at refining and perfecting your physical body and character (cleansing your body and mind), this effort will purify your Qi (Prana) so that you can achieve spiritual ascension. It instructs that you must cultivate your physical vitality or life force to attain the subtle body whose attainment then makes you an **"Earthly Immortal,"** which is the Taoist rank for the deva body achievement that is still bound to the earthly plane.

You work at cultivating, purifying, perfecting and transforming your internal energy so that what arises out of your physical body composed of Jing (semen) is an independent deva body composed of your purified subtle energy, or life force, called Qi or Prana. Taoism calls this an transmutation or transformation due to internal alchemy where your Qi has circulated throughout all of your body's energy meridians. This means that the process involves internal energy turning, churning, rotating and purifying. When you accomplish this, you become an Earthly Immortal.

Taoism uses the term "Immortal" to denote all its ranks of spiritual attainment, whereas Buddhism uses ranks of Arhatship, and the term "immortal" denotes the fact that these bodies have very long lives. The term "Immortal" in this context also signifies that the deva body is no longer bound by the normal cycle of birth and death because it can live for hundreds of years. The Greek story of Tiresias, *which actually refers to a man who attained the deva body stage of Arhatship*, says he was gifted with a lifespan of "seven ordinary lives." Basically, the term "Immortal" emphasizes the longevity, resilience, and transcendence of these spiritual bodies once they are attained.

When an Earthly Immortal continues to refine and purify their subtle body further, a new level of spiritual transformation occurs: the emergence of the Causal body out of the matrix of the subtle body. The Taoist term for this accomplishment is that one becomes a **"Spirit Immortal,"** where the term "spirit" also refers to Shen energy.

Shen is the name that Taoism gives to the life force energy of the subtle body that upon sufficient purification can leave the shell of the subtle body to become an independent life of its own, then making one a "Spirit Immortal." At this point, the practitioner possesses three interconnected bodies: the physical body (Jing), the subtle or deva body (Qi), and the Causal body (Shen). The Causal body now becomes the central vehicle of one's identity – the center of your life – while the lower bodies function as auxiliary shells or instruments.

If the practitioner continues to cultivate and purify their Causal body, they may attain the next, more exalted level of spiritual embodiment: the Supra-Causal body. Taoism refers to this attainment as becoming a **"Celestial Immortal."** This body is no longer defined by or confined by any of the lower realms and operates with a form and consciousness so refined that it corresponds to the Supra-Causal or Clear Light body, and is what Buddhism classifies as the Arhat's body. Taoism says that it dwells in heavenly realms, has the ability to appear in multiple forms, and is free from rebirth in the lower realms of being.

The Celestial Immortal can move freely across the celestial domains and exhibits profound spiritual abilities beyond the grasp of lower beings. Taoist texts explain that this stage of enlightenment has the ability to project *yang-shen*, which are tangible manifestations of one's spirit, and Taoist texts also say that such individuals can appear and disappear at will, which is yet another description of bilocation. As Zhang Sanfeng explained, one achieves the ability to appear in multiple places at once by cultivating one's internal energy because this leads to the attainment of the higher spiritual bodies. That cultivation is naturally produced by those who engage in ardent spiritual practices.

Finally, there is one more stage that lies beyond even this exalted state – a level of realization that understands one's unity with the fundamental substratum of the cosmos itself. Taoism refers to this stage of "attaining the Tao" as the **"Universal Immortal,"** which parallels the Perfect and Complete Enlightenment stage of Mahayana Buddhism that is equivalent to the Superconsciousness or Immanence body of Hindu cosmology. This is the realm of the "real man" or "true self" inside us who can manifest spontaneously because his detached mind abides nowhere, and follows no set pattern.

Thus, Taoism says that out of transformed Jing (the physical body) arises Qi (the subtle body), and out of transformed Qi arises Shen (the Causal body). Next, you work at refining and perfecting your Shen, which means the Causal body attainment equivalent to the Spirit Immortal, and by purifying the life force of that Shen body you can release a Supra-Causal body composed of what Taoism terms Later Heavenly Energy. This is when you become a "Celestial Immortal." If you then cultivate that Supra-Causal body and its life force, which is known as Primordial Heavenly Energy since it is the closest to our fundamental substratum, you can attain the highest spiritual attainment by becoming a "Universal Immortal," Great Golden Arhat and so forth. This is a simplification of the whole process.

To summarize: while our physical human body is composed of flesh and matter – originating from the union of egg and semen (known in Taoist terminology as Jing) – it is merely the outermost shell of a potential series of increasingly refined spiritual bodies that interpenetrate one another, but can become uncoupled if you cultivate internal energy purification and personal purity as well. Evil people will not attaint he help necessary to achieve these attainments.

The first higher body is composed of Qi, or vital energy, which animates our lives by supporting physiological and subtle functions. It is the internal vital energy that keeps us alive and which powers our consciousness. This subtle body of Qi – what many traditions call the energy body or deva body – serves as the foundation for further spiritual development.

Through diligent spiritual cultivation, it is possible to generate a higher body out of this Qi body: the Causal body, composed of Shen energy. This attainment corresponds to the Anagamin stage in Buddhism and the Spiritual Immortal stage in Taoism. Shen is often called the "life force of the mind" or "spirit" because it represents a more refined, smoother energy of consciousness than what Qi engenders. At this stage, consciousness becomes even more pristine than previously, and the body-mind continuum becomes increasingly liberated from any control exerted by the physical and subtle realms.

From within this Causal body, further purification can yield an even more exalted attainment: the Supra-Causal body, composed of what Taoism refers to as Later Heavenly Energy that is the purified life force of the Causal-bodied being. This marks the level of a full Arhat in Buddhism and a Celestial Immortal in the Taoist schema. The qualities of this body are so refined that many traditions describe it using metaphors such as light, rainbow, emptiness, formlessness, invisibility, or pure wisdom, as these evoke the body's non-material nature and limitless capabilities. It is beyond ordinary perception and is capable of traversing countless realms, manifesting *siddhis* (spiritual powers), and producing numerous emanations (*nirmanakayas*). This is the source of bilocation abilities, although even greater bilocation abilities are connected with the Superconsciousness body attainment.

The remaining work is the purification of this exalted body of Later Heavenly Energy so that a final body can be generated when its internal energy is purified. From within the Celestial Immortal's body – the Arhat's body composed of Later Heavenly Energy – an advanced adept can release the highest possible spiritual body: the Immanence Body, Superconsciousness body, Great Golden Arhat body, or Tathagata body. This final attainment represents the pure manifest *atman* or *jiva*, composed of Primordial Heavenly Energy. In Taoist language, this highest body is considered the "true human being" or *Zhenren* in Taoist terminology, for its core consciousness energy is closest to the ground state of consciousness that lies at the core of all sentient beings.

It is this level of realization that all spiritual traditions point to as the supreme goal of the path — not merely liberation, but full actualization of the purest divine nature of consciousness within. One does not become extinct, but still has existence, consciousness and experiences bliss.

CHRISTIANITY

The Christian reference to the higher bodies starts with Psalm 82:6, "Ye are gods," and 2 Corinthians 3:18, which says, "We all, with unveiled face, beholding the glory of the Lord, are being transformed into the same image from one degree of glory to another." To say that people are gods, or that there are stages of glory, are indirect ways of saying that there are progressively higher heavenly realms corresponding to stages of spiritual attainment, and the term "god" was used because the residents of the highest heavenly realms are typically called as such.

Furthermore, Jesus once said, "Truly, truly, I tell you, no one can see the Kingdom of Heaven unless he is born again." This means that you cannot see the Kingdom of Heaven until you achieve, at the barest minimum, the subtle body or deva body. To achieve this is like a second birth, although the birth is by transformation.

In Christianity, the angelic ranks also refer to the various spiritual bodies. These ranks, from highest to lowest, are the Seraphim, Cherubin, Thrones, Dominions, Virtues, Powers, Principalities, Archangels, and angels. These can be subdivided into rankings of purity and power that refer to the stages of the Superconsciousness, Supra-Casual, Causal and subtle body attainments.

Seraphim and Cherubin are naturally Superconsciousness-Immanence body attainees, while angels are subtle body beings. You can partition all nine of these rankings into the for upper transcendental body achievements. The process of *glorification, deification or divinization* in Christianity is simply the process of attaining these higher divine bodies by shedding the more materialistic shells that surround our highest manifest self-essence.

Basil of Alexandria said, "becoming a god is the highest goal of all," to indicate that the highest goal of Christianity is to attain these spiritual bodies. You do so by pursuing religious practices that involve purifying yourself and becoming a more virtuous individual. The Church Father Athanasius of Alexandria said, "He (Jesus) was made human so that he might make us gods," which also refers to this spiritual ladder of ascension, while the Church Father Clement of Alexandria assured us, "he who obeys the Lord and follows the prophecy given through him ... becomes a god while still moving about in the flesh."

The meaning of these quotes is that Jesus's teachings and the path he laid out, when followed, would enable you to attain the subtle body that is the first stage of spiritual ascension. You can attain the subtle body while living, "while still moving about in the flesh," as the saints of many traditions have accomplished, and Christianity is just one among many proven pathways for accomplishing this spiritual goal. It is a great tragedy that many modern people have abandoned regular attendance at Christian church services because this is when higher spiritual beings regularly wash, in minor fashion, the Prana of each parishioner in a flock to help keep people healthy and balanced.

Clement of Alexandria said, "Yea, I say, the Word of God became a man so that you might learn from a man how to become a god," which is the basis of Christianity. Saint Athanasius said, "He was incarnate that we might be made god," which also tells people that by following the Christian path they can attain these higher bodies and ascend through glorification.

St. Thomas Aquinas also wrote, "The only-begotten Son of God, wanting to make us sharers in his divinity, assumed our nature, so that he, made man, might make men gods." The reason Jesus came down, he was saying, is to give us a path that we can follow to ascend by attaining the higher bodies of deification. Therefore Saint Irenaeus also stated, "the Word became man, and the Son of God became the Son of man so that man, by entering into communion with the Word and thus receiving divine sonship, might become a son of God."

CONCLUSION

By referencing several major religions, we have established that most of them recognize that spiritual saints possess five spiritual bodies.

Hinduism reveals that each of these bodies functions like a disposable shell and identified the abilities of the deva body (eight *siddhi*), which are emphasized in the schools of Yoga.

Sufism (Islam) explains how the five planes of existence formed, with bodies developing on each plane. Each plane is considered a densification of its predecessor.

Druze, Sikhism and Judaism also acknowledge the existence of the five bodies and five separate planes of existence.

Taoism explains the different levels of energies that compose each spiritual body. It also explains how the energies of each body are gradually differentiated from each other – an "alchemical" process of transmutation – because of virtuous behavior and *nei-gong* internal energy exercises. The energies become highly purified through spiritual practices, and thus gradually become distinctly differentiated from the grossness of their host body and its untransformed animalistic energy. Because of the distinctive purity achieved through this personal cultivation effort, a new divine body can arise from an older body vehicle.

Confucianism explains the general process for cultivating the higher bodies, and particularly noted the loftiness of the fourth and fifth levels of attainment.

Buddhism offers the most comprehensive information on the five bodies and their correspondence to other ranking schemes for spiritual attainment. It explains that bilocation demonstrates the *nirmanakaya* abilities of the Arhat (Supra-Causal body) or Great Golden Arhat (Superconsciousness body) stages of attainment. While Taoism simply explains that there exists a stage when bilocation becomes possible, and provides details on how to cultivate such stages, it does not offer the finer details that Buddhism provides.

The attainment of these bodies is a non-sectarian, non-denominational result that runs across all the genuine religions, as you have seen. The genuine world religions and spiritual paths are just different ways to accomplish this feat, which they all recognize as a lofty achievement and the *actual purpose of religion*, in addition to its function of producing peace, cooperation and behavioral order in society. The problem is that few religions provide much information on this ladder because they know that very few people can achieve this ascension during life, and therefore they don't want to discourage people from spiritual ways, which would certainly happen if people commonly knew the accomplishment was so difficult.

For the topic of this book, we need to draw attention to the fact that only the fourth and fifth bodies are capable of bilocation. In Buddhist terms, these are the Arhat and Great Golden Arhat bodies, or the Supra-Casual and Immanence (Superconsciousness) bodies in Hinduism. All the individuals mentioned in Chapter One achieved these bodies to perform the materialization of a spiritual body in another location.

The spiritual saints previously mentioned in our first chapter could perform bilocation because they had achieved, through spiritual practices, the casting off of lower physical shells to attain the higher bodies capable of *nirmanakaya* projections, which every religion has stated is a lofty stage of spiritual achievement. Once attained, they must master the ability to condense the energy of a higher body, or one of its *nirmanakaya* emanations, in a tangible materialization so that it can be seen and touched. This is what people witness during bilocation events.

Any spiritual master who reaches the stage of the Arhat can perform bilocation and other miracles, but as a rule, spiritual masters of most sects usually don't demonstrate their superpowers. One way to suspect whether an individual may have "become enlightened" and achieved this multi-body status is that they are appointed as the guiding head of a lineage or tradition with a long track record of enlightened sages. This includes some Sangharaja in Theravada Buddhism, some of the Shankaracharyas of India, some Sufi Sheikhs, some Jewish Chief rabbis or Hasidic dynasty leaders, Christians who became canonized as saints by the Catholic or Eastern Orthodox Church, and so forth.

Of course, an enlightened individual will usually deny that they have become enlightened or achieved these bodies, but when a guru sits motionless "in *samadhi*" for extended periods of time, it is not because his mind is empty, free of thoughts. Rather, it is usually *because his spiritual bodies have left to traverse the world*, which is why many masters go into secluded retreat so that they can often do this without getting disturbed. Masters usually hide the fact that their spiritual bodies were absent traveling elsewhere by saying they were personally absorbed in a thoughtless *samadhi* experience, or that they were experiencing some type of communion or ecstasy with God.

When the Hindu saint Ramakrishna would sit motionless "in trance," some students thought his mind was in some beatific *samadhi*, but he was just absent from his physical shell, traveling about in his higher spiritual bodies. They believed his motionless body had to be fed or he would perish but this was simply ignorance on their part.

As two other examples, during the process of achieving their final Superconsciousness body attainment, both Milarepa and Shakyamuni Buddha would leave their human body alone for days without food as their higher spirits traveled elsewhere to obtain the assistance required to ascend higher once again. They ignored the health of their human body's deplorable condition because it really doesn't matter anymore once someone starts achieving the highest possible bodies. For instance, the Christian saint Pade Pio frequently said, "After my death I will do more. My real mission will begin after my death." This is because after discarding his physical body he could then devote all his time to using his higher bodies to help people.

Related to this, Sufi Sheikh Muhammed Hisham Kabbani stated clearly in *The Hierarchy of Saints* that the enlightened often travel from their locations, leaving their bodies behind to help people who need assistance, and their bodies remain motionless during their absence so you should not disturb them. Chinese Buddhism and Taoism also instruct us never to touch those bodies in deep meditation. You certainly should not pull on them or shake them in any way, but can call back a master's spirit by ringing a chime next to their ear. Usually when a master is sleeping his body is roaming the world as well, so the same warning holds.

Another method is to find individuals who gradually climbed the ranks of a tradition to reach its highest levels, such as attaining the Great Schema monastic rank of the Eastern Orthodox Church, whose membership level includes:

Saint Anthony the Great (c. 251-356) – Father of All Christian Monks
Saint Pachomius the Great (292-348) – the first to invest monks with the
    full monastic dignity of the schema
Saint Jonah of Kiev (1802-1902) – Russian Orthodox Schema Monk
Saint Pachomius the Great (c. 292-348) – Founder of Cenobitic
    Monasticism
Saint Seraphim of Sarov (1754-1833) – Russian Orthodox Schema Monk

Saint Charbel Makhlouf (1828-1898) – Lebanese Maronite Schema Monk
Saint Silouan the Athonite (1866-1938) – Schema Monk of Mount Athos
Saint John of Shanghai and San Francisco (1896-1966) – Wonderworker Russian Monk
Saint Paisios of Mount Athos (1924-1994) – Greek Orthodox Schema Monk
Saint Herman of Alaska (c. 1756-1837) – Russian Orthodox Schema Monk
Saint Sergius of Radonezh (1314-1392) – Russian Orthodox Schema Monk
Saint Macarius the Great (c. 300-391) – Egyptian Desert Father
Saint Isaac the Syrian (c. 640-700) – Schema Monk and Theologian
Saint Nil Sorsky (1433-1508) – Russian Orthodox Schema Monk
Saint Arsenius the Great (354-449) – Desert Father and Schema Monk
Saint Maximus the Confessor (580-662) – Theologian and Schema Monk
Saint Mary of Egypt (c. 344-421) – Schema Nun
Saint Theophan the Recluse (1815-1894) – Russian Orthodox Hieroschemamonk
Saint Symeon the New Theologian (949-1022) – Byzantine Schema Monk
Saint Gabriel of Georgia (Urgebadze) (1929-1995) – Georgian Orthodox Schema Monk

Many of these individuals demonstrated miracles during their lifetime, which lends further credence to the assumption that they achieved the higher transcendental body attainments. This accomplishment makes them worthy of veneration or prayers seeking their help. Whenever any individual, of any religion, achieves such a lofty attainment it is common for them to be venerated by the public and receive prayers of supplication asking for assistance for various affairs. This is the idea behind praying to saints and spiritual masters for guidance and assistance.

CHAPTER 3:
PROVEN CASES OF INCORRUPTIBLE BODIES

Having established that bilocation comes from the attainment of higher spiritual bodies, which can somehow materialize into our physical world by condensing energy into particles, we next have to deal with the phenomenon of incorruptibility. Incorruptibility is often seen in the bodies of the very same saints who demonstrated bilocation or other spiritual gifts such as wonderworking miracles.

The phenomenon of incorruptibility is when a person's body is preserved after death by not naturally decaying or decomposing. When only part of a person's body is preserved from decomposition after death (e.g. tongue, heart, hand) it is considered "partially incorrupt."

First, let us address the cause of this phenomenon.

Second, let us once again show that uncorrupted bodies are a *non-denominational phenomenon* that has happened to the bodies of many people who strongly cultivated a spiritual path regardless of their religion. The saints or sages of many religions have demonstrated incorruptibility after death so it is definitely a non-sectarian phenomenon, but unfortunately people usually cling to their own sectarian bias.

Taoism explains that the process of cultivating the higher spiritual bodies entails purifying your inner vital energy, which is the life force of your body known as Qi or Prana. This vital energy belongs to the subtle body inside you – your spirit that arises after death – which is what keeps you alive. By churning your vital energy in various ways by guiding it with your mind, which is a process Taoism calls *nei-gong* or *neijia*, you can start purifying this inner energy on demand. The process of churning, revolving or rotating your internal energy causes friction, and that friction causes heat and its purification. However, there are times when you will feel coolness, or even tremendous cold without your own doing.

Many spiritual practitioners do not do *nei-gong* exercises at all where they lead their internal energy inside themselves using their mind. This is most commonly taught in eastern spiritual paths like Buddhism, Taoism, Hinduism, Tantra, Yoga, Shugendo, Shingon, and so forth.

What usually happens to people who deeply, ardently devote themselves to religious practices is that this process automatically, unexpectedly appears within them after they apply themselves to deep religious practices. It just spontaneously occurs. A churning of energies, or waves of undulating energy from head to toe, begins to be felt in their body, accompanied by great heat or sometimes cold, and often by great pain or discomfort. Then these revolutions of energy inside their body continue for years, thereby purifying its tissues so that their bodies don't deteriorate after death, but this only happens to individuals performing intense spiritual practice. It is this purification process lasting many years, where the energies rotating inside yourself cleanse every tissue of your body, that produces an incorruptible body.

For instance, Christian monks and mystics throughout history have frequently reported experiencing powerful physical sensations during intense prayer and ascetic practices, particularly strong currents of energy and extreme sensations of heat or cold. These phenomena have been documented across centuries of Christian mystical tradition, notably in the histories of Christian saints regardless of their tradition. They were frequently interpreted as manifestations of divine presence or spiritual purification, both of which are correct in some sense. While Christians interpret this as the workings of the Holy Spirit, the eastern religions simply call this a "kundalini awakening" and explain that this is the process of purifying your vital (subtle) energy along with your physical body. In Christianity this is the actual process of *deification, divinization or glorification* by which you attain the purified spiritual subtle body as a result of your merit, efforts to purify your conduct and spiritual efforts.

Perhaps the most famous modern example is **Padre Pio**, who experienced such intense heat during his spiritual exercises that he frequently needed to open windows even in winter or use fans to cool himself. This burning sensation was so pronounced that those near him could sometimes feel the heat radiating from his body. Bishop Rossi, who investigated his case, learned that Father Lorenzo of San Marco had personally witnessed Padre Pio with fevers of 109.4 degrees Fahrenheit, then 113 degrees, and finally a sizzling 118.4 degrees – way beyond what causes fatality in normal humans. A temperature of 107 degrees for several hours is known to kill even healthy teenagers. At other times it soared even higher. Sometimes Padre Pio would have fevers so high that the doctor had to use a veterinary thermometer for horses to measure his temperature because ordinary thermometers would break because his body was so hot.

Saint Catherine of Genoa would become so inflamed with "divine love" that she needed to lie on the cold ground to find relief when she went through this process. The Polish Catholic nun, Sister Maria Faustina, also wrote of her own kundalini experiences, saying, "I was all afire, but without burning up ... I felt some kind of fire in my heart ... I was so enveloped in the great interior fire of God's love ... I feel I am all aflame. ... Today, a living flame of divine love entered my soul."[4]

Similarly, the 14th-century English mystic Richard Rolle (the Hermit of Hampole) wrote of being consumed by a "fire of love" that overwhelmed his body with warmth during spiritual contemplation, which he interpreted as a tangible manifestation of God's presence. He wrote,

> It was real warmth, too, and it felt as if it were actually on fire. I was astonished at the way the heat surged up, and how this new sensation brought great and unexpected comfort. I had to keep feeling my breast to make sure there was no physical reason for it! But once I realized that it came entirely from within, that this fire of love had no cause, material or sinful, but was the gift of my Maker, I was absolutely delighted, and wanted my love to be even greater. ... If we put our finger near a fire we feel the heat; in much the same way a soul on fire with love feels, I say, a genuine warmth.[5]

---

[4] *Mystics of the Christian Tradition*, Steven Fanning, (Routledge, London, 2001), p. 205.
[5] *The Fire of Love*, Richard Rolle, trans. by Clifton Wolters, (Penguin, Baltimore, 1972), pp. 88-89.

Fire, warmth, and heat – often interpreted as mystical love, divine warmth, or *incendium amoris* – was also reported by St. Augustine, Bernard of Clairvaux, Hildegard of Bingen, Symeon the New Theologian, Theophan the Recluse, John Tauler, Angela of Foligno, Francisco de Osuna, Margery Kempe, Marie of the Incarnation, Madame Guyon, George Fox, William Law, and even Blaise Pascal.[6] In Steven Fanning's book, *Mystics of the Christian Tradition*, you can read about all sorts of similar phenomena experienced by various Christian saints.

If you want a broader spectrum of all sorts of phenomena you can turn to *Meditation Case Studies: Concise Explanations of Phenomena Encountered on the Spiritual Path*. One basic principle you will discover is that "Moving Warmth = Purification."

For Hinduism, Sri Ramakrishna Paramahamsa reported that he experienced serpent-like energy in his spine for years during this transformation process, as well as burning heat, tremors, ecstatic fits and visions of divine deities or light. One particular narrative concerning the Hindus sage Ramana Maharshi describes an instance where, overwhelmed by this inner fire, he entered the inner sanctum of the Arunachaleswara Temple where, in a moment of deep devotion and surrender, he embraced its Shiva Linga. This act is said to have brought about a profound sense of relief and peace, effectively calming the intense energy that had been surging within him *for years*.

The Desert Fathers, including **Saint Anthony the Great** (251-356) and **Saint Macarius of Egypt** (300-391), wrote of experiencing both burning heat and freezing cold during their spiritual warfare, and interpreted these sensations as either divine consolations or demonic attacks. The Japanese Zen monk **Hakuin Ekaku** (1686-1769), also wrote of his limbs feeling freezing cold (you can find his highly recommended story in *A Second Zen Reader*, retitled *The Tiger's Cave*, by Trevor Leggett) and came up with spiritual exercises for solving the problem that we will later reveal.

Saint John of the Cross (1542-1591) described the "living flame of love" that would burn within the soul during mystical union, while **Saint Teresa of Avila** (1515-1582) wrote of experiencing "transverberation" – a burning sensation as if her heart were pierced by a flaming arrow.

---

[6] *Mystics of the Christian Tradition*, Steven Fanning, (Routledge, London, 2001), pp. 217-218.

The intense states of heat were sometimes accompanied by fevers, trembling, or a sensation of liquid fire coursing throughout the body. The heat was often seen by Christian recipients as a purifying force that burned away sin and worldly attachments, while cold was assumed to signify a different kind of divine presence, as seen in some accounts of mystical encounters. This process entails streams of energy rolling around your body, or passing through it in waves, and this happens daily for years. This is often accompanied by visionary experiences or intense emotional experiences, which will be explained later.

The theological understanding of these phenomena varies within the various Christian traditions. Some interpret these sensations as direct manifestations of the Holy Spirit, similar to the "tongues of fire" described at Pentecost. Others view them as simply psychosomatic responses to intense spiritual practices, while still maintaining their significance as signs of genuine spiritual transformation. In the Eastern Orthodox tradition, these experiences are often associated with the activation of the "noetic faculty" or spiritual heart, while Western mystics frequently link them to the stages of mystical union.

Despite the different explanations in Christianity that are essentially guesswork, the consistency of these reports across cultures and centuries suggests a genuine mystical phenomenon – of a profound actual *physical nature* – that accompanies deep states of prayer and contemplation, serving as a reminder of the profound connection between body and spirit in spiritual metaphysics. What these individuals experienced was not fantasy but actual experience.

What also remains consistent across the highly documented accounts in the Christian traditions is a common understanding that these physical manifestations, while dramatic, are somehow signs of the purification and transformation of the soul. Now that we have access to the more detailed explanations from eastern religions, we can understand that they are simply part of the process that purifies the inner energies of one's subtle body so that through purification it becomes more differentiated from its lower nature and physical counterparts, and can thus become detached from the body shell as the bonds weaken. Once the bonds weaken sufficiently, it can escape its physical prison as an independent life.

The eastern religions explain that it takes a minimum of twelve years of such purifying transformations before the subtle body can be released, and usually several years longer. Because of the troubles involved when going through this process, most eastern religions see that it happens to a worthy recipient under the watchful eyes of a monk or nun who already achieved enlightenment (the higher spiritual body attainments). The expectation is that the neophyte will one day become the spiritual head of that religious sect, or some type of spiritual successor (such as the head abbot of a temple or monastery somewhere) who helps carry on the tradition.

Whether interpreted as divine energy, the Holy Spirit's descent, the soul's fiery longing for God, or as the more accurate eastern explanations of one's vital energy being purified during the process of kundalini purification via the assistance of other enlightened saints and spiritual masters, in Christianity these physical manifestations reinforced the monks' beliefs that spiritual prayer was not merely a mental exercise but a transformative encounter with the sacred on the path to holiness.

Typically we find the most verified cases of incorruptibility in the Christian and Buddhist traditions. One of the reasons we don't find more cases in other religions is because in some traditions the corpse is burned, in which case *sariras* or relics are often left behind instead of a body. In other traditions the bodies are rarely exhumed after burial, so no one can discover their sacred nature. In yet other instances, the weather is so detrimental in that location that even a purified body will experience some degree of deterioration after death.

To acquaint you with the non-denominational nature of this phenomenon, we will provide a short list of some notable spiritual greats who left behind incorruptible bodies cleansed by the kundalini purification process, which eastern religions thereafter call "whole body relics," and will show, whenever possible, that most every one of these individuals devoted themselves to intensive spiritual practices. This is a prerequisite for spiritual attainments.

Naturally this list of examples is biased in numbers to examples from Christianity and Buddhism because of the great preponderance of their cases, though it has also been seen for practitioners of Taoism, Hinduism, and other religions. This must be the case, for it is a *non-denominational result* of the kundalini spiritual purification process.

CHRISTIANITY: WITNESSES TO TRANSFORMATION

The Catholic author Joan Carroll Cruz's book, *The Incorruptibles (2021)*, states there are an estimated 100 incorrupt saints that the Catholic church officially recognizes so we will list just a few of these other saints. The majority of incorrupt saints come from Italy, but a large number of incorrupt saints also came from France.

Most of the cases we find are of canonized figures, often exhumed for beautification whereupon their incorrupt body is discovered, which is sometimes months or years after their death. The first-known incorrupt saint is **Saint Cecilia**, who died in Rome around 177 AD[7] and her incorrupt body was discovered over 1,500 years later!

The hearts, tongues or bones often remain for some saints while the rest decays, and many remains emit a sweet fragrance that reminds people of specific flowers. This is all confirmed by the Church before it announces that a saint's body shows signs of incorruption. In certain instances, partially incorrupt saints retain a life-like face that has resisted decomposition, but the skin on their hands appears less preserved than other areas of the body. This is due to less purification of these regions over an individual's lifetime.

Of course, not all incorrupt Christian bodies are saints of the Catholic tradition. Orthodox Christian saints – as well as Hindus, Taoists and even Buddhist monks – have confirmed cases of incorrupt bodies after they were exhumed. To complicate matters, not all saints have incorrupt bodies either.

Here are some of these cases, starting with individuals from Roman Catholicism, and once again note the non-denominational character of the phenomenon and the fact that the saint engaged in extensive spiritual practices: Let's start off again with Padre Pio.

The body of **St. Pio of Pietrelcina** (**Padre Pio**, 1887–1968) showed minimal decay when exhumed in 2008 (forty years after his death), and is now displayed in San Giovanni Rotondo for all to see as just another example proving the truth of incorruptibility. His body is described as being in "fair condition," with the upper skull partially skeletal but the chin and hands well-preserved, though a silicone mask covers his face due to deterioration.

---

[7] Giovanni Battista de Rossi argues that she passed away in Sicily between 176 and 180 AD though some sources place her martyrdom around 230 AD.

Padre Pio practiced intense prayer, fasting, and Eucharistic devotion, often spending hours in confession and celebrating Mass with profound reverence. He was renowned for miracles, including healing the sick, reading souls, and bearing the stigmata for fifty years, with accounts of levitation and supernatural fragrance coming from his wounds. Bilocation was well-documented, with credible reports of him appearing in distant locations, such as hospitals or battlefields, while physically remaining in San Giovanni Rotondo. His relics continue to inspire pilgrims, with many people reporting healings at his shrine.

St. Francis of Assisi's (1181–1226) body, when exhumed in 1918, was found intact and fragrant after 600 years. It is now enshrined in the Basilica of St. Francis (Assisi). During his life St. Francis also exhibited the stigmata of Christ just like Padre Pio, receiving the stigmata in 1224 that was considered a divine mark of Christ's wounds. His body remains remarkably preserved, though some accounts note minor decay, and there is a sweet odor emanating from the relics. St. Francis practiced extreme asceticism, including fasting, poverty, and constant prayer, often retreating to Mount La Verna for contemplation. He was known for miracles such as taming a wolf or preaching to birds. No definitive accounts of bilocation exist, though his spiritual influence was felt widely across Italy during his lifetime. His incorrupt relics continue to draw countless pilgrims every year.

In France, **St. John Vianney** (1786–1859), who would know people's sins during confession (one of the Six Supernatural Powers mentioned by Buddhism) and produced the miracle of multiplying food, had his body exhumed in 1904, whereupon it was found intact. It is now enshrined at Ars. His body, while largely preserved, is covered with a wax mask due to slight facial deterioration, maintaining a lifelike appearance. St. John practiced rigorous fasting, minimal sleep, and hours of prayer, dedicating up to 16 hours daily to hearing confessions. He performed miracles, including multiplying bread for orphans and clairvoyantly discerning penitents' sins, earning him fame as the "Curé d'Ars." His relics continue to inspire devotion, with pilgrims reporting spiritual transformations at his shrine.

The body of **St. Thérèse of Lisieux** (1873–1897), "The Little Flower," are not fully incorrupt, but her heart and bones are preserved as relics at the Basilica of Lisieux. While her body showed some decay upon exhumation, the relics remain remarkably preserved, with a sweet floral scent readily noted by pilgrims. She practiced intense prayer, fasting, and her "Little Way" of spiritual childhood, offering small acts for God. Miracles attributed to her include healing a blind child and numerous posthumous intercessions, earning her the title "Doctor of the Church."

St. Bernadette of Lourdes (1844-1879), the visionary who witnessed eighteen apparitions of the Virgin Mary at Lourdes, France, lived a life marked by extraordinary spiritual intensity following her mystical experiences at the age of 14. She was known for eighteen apparitions of the Virgin Mary in 1858, leading to the miraculous healing spring at Lourdes. After the Marian apparitions ended in 1858, Bernadette joined the Sisters of Charity of Nevers, adopting a life of profound prayer, humility, and self-sacrifice. Born Marie-Bernarde Soubirous in Lourdes (not Germany), she spent her final 13 years at the Convent of St. Gildard in Nevers, where she developed a reputation for heroic contemplative prayer, often spending hours in chapel practicing mental prayer and Eucharistic adoration.

Following her death on April 16, 1879, at age 35, Bernadette's body was buried in the cemetery of the Convent of St. Gildard without any embalming or special preservation techniques. The remarkable preservation of her remains became evident during her first exhumation on September 22, 1909, exactly thirty years after her death, when church officials found her body virtually intact, with only slight darkening of the face and hands. A detailed medical examination revealed that her internal organs remained uncorrupted, her muscles retained elasticity, and her skin, though somewhat darkened, showed no signs of decomposition.

During her second exhumation in 1919, forty years post-mortem, physicians found her body had remained basically unchanged, with the surprising observation that her liver had actually turned white but remained perfectly preserved – a phenomenon medical experts could not explain. Her third and final exhumation occurred in 1925, when her body was transferred to a glass reliquary at the Convent of St. Gildard, where it remains on public display to this day. Scientific examinations confirmed no artificial preservation methods had been employed, and her state of preservation continues to defy medical explanation.

The Church views Bernadette's incorruption as a physical sign of her sanctity, reflecting the remarkable interior purity she had cultivated through her contemplative practice and mystical union with God following her visions at Lourdes. Her incorrupt relics at the Convent of St. Gildard (in Nevers, France) draw millions, with ongoing miracles reported at Lourdes.

The incorrupt body of another Italian stigmatic, **St. Rita of Cascia** (1381–1457), sits upright in a glass urn at Cascia Basilica (located in the Umbria region of central Italy), still wearing her habit. Amazingly, her stigmata wound still "bleeds" annually. Her body remains remarkably preserved, with flexible limbs and a fragrant odor, though slight wax enhancements maintain her appearance. St. Rita practiced intense prayer, fasting, and penance, living as an Augustinian nun after a difficult marriage, often meditating on Christ's Passion. She was known for miracles, including the annual bleeding of her stigmata wound and the miraculous growth of roses in winter. Her incorrupt relics draw thousands, with the bleeding stigmata considered a sign of ongoing miracles.

The body of **Blessed Anna Maria Taigi** (1769–1837), Trinitarian tertiary and visionary who could predict the future, resisted decay for months in Rome's summer heat. It is now resting in the San Crisogono Church located in Rome, Italy. Her remains, while largely intact, show some natural decay but retain a remarkable state, often described as fragrant by early witnesses. She practiced daily prayer, fasting, and acts of charity, balancing family life with mystical visions of a glowing orb revealing future events. Her miracles included accurate prophecies, such as predicting papal elections, and healing the sick through prayer. No definitive accounts of bilocation exist, though her visions allowed her to perceive distant events spiritually. Her relics continue to inspire devotion, particularly among Trinitarians.

The body of **St. Charbel** (**Charbel Makhlouf,** 1828–1898), a Lebanese Maronite monk, showed no decay when exhumed in 2020. Multiple exhumations documented the preservation of his body over several decades. During his life, he developed a reputation for holiness and tried to unite Christians, Muslims and Druze. Four months after his death in December 1898, mysterious lights were seen above his tomb for forty-five nights prompting ecclesiastical authorities to open it whereupon they found his body still intact despite the grave being flooded with rainwater and the corpse floating in mud. A blood-like liquid was observed flowing from the body, and monks had to change his garments twice weekly due to staining. Experts and doctors were unable to give medical explanations for the incorruptibility and flexibility.

In 1950 and 1952, his tomb was officially opened and his body still had the appearance of a living one as documented by medical committees. Additionally, the 1950 television tape of his exhumation showed Makhlouf's body as still intact, despite the grave having become severely rusty. In this century his grave has been opened four times, the last time being in 1955, and each time it has been noticed that his bleeding body still has its flexibility as if it were alive. Father Joseph Mahfouz certified that in 1965 the body of Saint Charbel was still preserved intact with no alteration. However, in 1976, he again witnessed the opening of the grave, but this time the body was completely decomposed with only the skeleton remaining.

During her life, **St. Catherine Labouré** (1806–1876) of France saw many Marian apparitions, and was known for making accurate prophecies. Her body has not decayed since 1876 and is displayed in a glass reliquary, 140+ years after death, at Chapelle Notre-Dame de la Médaille Miraculeuse de Paris. Her remains are remarkably intact, with flexible limbs and minimal deterioration, enhanced by a thin wax coating. She practiced intense prayer, fasting, and devotion to the Virgin Mary, living humbly as a Daughter of Charity. Her miracles include the 1830 Marian apparitions leading to the Miraculous Medal and accurate prophecies about French political upheavals. Her incorrupt relics draw pilgrims, with many reporting healings through the Miraculous Medal.

Two modern popes (Pius X and John XXIII) are both canonized and widely recognized as having incorruptible bodies, thus indicating that they had done many spiritual practices during their life and gone through some of the necessary processes of spiritual transformation for the heavenly reward of higher spiritual bodies.

The first is **Pope St. Pius X** (1835–1914), whose body was found in a remarkably preserved state when exhumed in 1944, thirty years after his death. It is now displayed in a glass reliquary in St. Peter's Basilica. His body remains largely intact, with minimal decay and a slight fragrance noted by early examiners, though some wax enhancement aids veneration. He practiced daily prayer, Eucharistic devotion, and simplicity, emphasizing catechesis and liturgical reform as pope. His relics continue to inspire devotion, particularly for his humility and piety.

When the tomb of **Pope St. John XXIII** (1881–1963) was opened in 2001, his body was found in a surprisingly intact state. His remains, preserved with minimal decay, are displayed in St. Peter's Basilica, with a lifelike appearance enhanced by wax to cover slight deterioration. He practiced fervent prayer, fasting, and charity, maintaining humility despite his papal role, and was known for initiating Vatican II. Miracles attributed to him include healing a dying woman during his lifetime and posthumous healings during his canonization process. His relics draw pilgrims for veneration, with many attributing spiritual graces to his intercession.

Two American incorruptibles include **St. Elizabeth Ann Seton** (1774–1821), the first U.S.-born saint, whose body, exhumed in 1901, was largely intact after eighty years; now enshrined in a bronze casket at the National Shrine (Emmitsburg, Maryland). Her remains, while showing some decay, retain remarkable preservation, with a faint, sweet fragrance reported by early examiners. She practiced daily prayer, Eucharistic devotion, and acts of charity, founding the Sisters of Charity and America's first Catholic schools. Miracles attributed to her include healing a child of acute lymphatic leukemia and curing a 4-year old boy of lymphoma affecting multiple organs during her canonization process.

The body of **Ven. Fulton Sheen** (1895–1979), the second American, showed minimal decay when exhumed in 2019 (cause for beatification). His remains, while not fully incorrupt, are remarkably preserved, with soft tissue intact, and are venerated as a sign of holiness. He practiced daily Eucharistic adoration, fasting, and preaching, gaining fame through radio and television evangelization. His relics in Peoria, Illinois, draw pilgrims, with ongoing miracles reported through his intercession.

Mary MacKillop (1842–1909), Australia's first saint, had her tomb exhumed in 1993 for beatification. Though not fully incorrupt, her remains were found remarkably intact (skin, hair, and skeletal structure intact) despite being buried 92 years in a damp wooden coffin. A faint floral scent was noted. She practiced daily prayer, fasting, and charity, and founded the Sisters of St. Joseph to educate the poor. Miracles attributed to her include healing a woman of leukemia and curing a child of brain cancer during her canonization process (after a nun prayed to MacKillop). Her relics in Sydney draw pilgrims, with ongoing miracles reported through her intercession.

Jose Gregorio Hernandez (1864–1919) was a Venezuelan physician, scientist, and devout Catholic who became widely known as the "Doctor of the Poor" for his tireless service to the sick and needy, especially during times of disease outbreaks and economic hardship. Renowned for integrating his deep spiritual life with his medical vocation, Hernández offered free treatment to those who could not afford it and was often seen praying by his patients' bedsides. He maintained a disciplined life of daily Mass, prayer, fasting, and acts of charity, and even studied for the priesthood before returning to medicine by necessity.

After his sudden death in a car accident in Caracas in 1919, public veneration for Hernández rapidly grew. His body, though naturally exhibiting some signs of decay, has remained remarkably well-preserved and is considered incorrupt by many due to the minimal decomposition – especially given the environmental conditions. His remains are housed in the Church of Our Lady of Candelaria in Caracas, where thousands come each year to seek healing or offer thanks. Countless testimonies from across Venezuela and Latin America credit miraculous healings and medical recoveries to his intercession, and reports of posthumous apparitions, including visions during surgeries or in hospital rooms, have added to his mystique and popular sainthood.

Another surgeon, **St. Luka** (1877-1961), provides us an introduction to Orthodox Christianity as he was canonized by the Russian Orthodox Church. Born Luke Voyno-Yasenetsky, he is now known as Luke of Simferopol or Saint Luke of Crimea. He was a Russian surgeon, spiritual writer, a bishop of the Russian Orthodox Church, and archbishop of Simferopol and Crimea. Despite living under an atheistic regime that actively persecuted religious figures, he openly practiced his faith, preached the Gospel, and continued his medical work even while facing arrest, exile, and imprisonment under Stalin's regime. Known posthumously as St. Luke the Blessed Surgeon, he is revered not only for his groundbreaking contributions to medicine, particularly in the field of purulent surgery, but also for his spiritual writings and the courage he showed in preserving Orthodox Christian teachings in hostile times.

On March 17, 1996, Luke's remains were disinterred, with many thousands of people attending the ceremony. Witnesses reported that an indescribable fragrance, often considered a sign of sanctity in Orthodox hagiography, emanated from his remains., while his heart was discovered incorrupt. Just three days later, on March 20, 1996, his relics were transferred to their final resting place in the Cathedral of the Holy Trinity in Simferopol, where they continue to draw pilgrims from around the Orthodox world. St. Luke was formally canonized in 2000 by the Ukrainian Orthodox Church under the Moscow Patriarchate. Today, he is venerated as a patron of surgeons and the sick, with many accounts of miraculous healings attributed to his intercession.

EASTERN ORTHODOX CHRISTIANITY

Now turning to Eastern Orthodox Christianity, we find a number of confirmed cases of incorruptibility.

St. Spyridon of Trimythous (270–348), Bishop of Trimythous (Cyprus/Greece), is known to have raised the dead, healed Emperor Constantius II by touch, and commanded nature by praying for rain to end a severe drought in Cyprus. His entire body remains intact after 1,700+ years, with flexible limbs and a warm temperature, enshrined in Corfu. Miraculously, his shoes wear out yearly – believed to "walk" performing miracles. St. Spyridon practiced fervent prayer, fasting, and humility, often spending nights in vigil. He was renowned for miracles, and defended Orthodoxy at the First Council of Nicaea by making a clay brick shoot out fire from its top and drip water from below. When soldiers came to arrest him during persecution, Spyridon crossed a river as if on dry land, leaving his pursuers stunned. Accounts of bilocation exist, with reports of him appearing to save sailors during storms while his body remained in Corfu. His relics continue to exude a sweet fragrance, reinforcing his sanctity.

The body of **St. Nektarios of Aegina** (1846–1920), exhumed in 1923, was found intact and emitting myrrh, now at Holy Trinity Monastery

(Aegina). His relics remain flexible and preserved, with a sweet scent reported by pilgrims. St. Nektarios was known for daily prayer, fasting, and writing theological works, living a life of humility despite persecution. He performed numerous miracles, including healing cancer patients and aiding the poor, with many miracles reported posthumously at his shrine. Bilocation accounts exist, such as his appearance in a remote village during Paschal services, as noted by villagers in Aegina. After his death the nuns of the monastery he built said that he walked its halls, prayed with the nuns there and offered them guidance. His incorrupt body continues to draw thousands seeking healing and spiritual guidance.

The famous Russian monk, **St. Seraphim of Sarov** (1754–1833), was known for prophecy and healing miracles. Exhumed in 1903, his body was uncorrupted and fragrant, and is now at Diveyevo Monastery. His remains, though partially decayed in some accounts, retain a remarkable state with a sweet odor, venerated as a sign of sanctity. St. Seraphim practiced intense asceticism, including prolonged prayer on a rock for 1,000 nights and strict fasting. He was renowned for miracles like healing the sick and foretelling events, such as the recovery of a nobleman's daughter. His relics continue to inspire miracles, drawing pilgrims to Diveyevo.

St. Dionysios of Zakynthos (1547–1622) was known for miraculously calming storms and saving Greek sailors during his life. His incorruptible body remains flexible and fragrant, enshrined in St. Dionysios Church (Zakynthos) and paraded annually on his feast day (August 24). The relics are remarkably preserved, with reports of seaweed found at his feet and worn-out slippers, suggesting that he "walks" to perform miracles and aid believers. St. Dionysios was known for intense prayer, fasting, and acts of forgiveness, famously sparing his brother's murderer. St. Dionysios practiced rigorous fasting, nightly prayer, and acts of charity, notably forgiving his brother's murderer. He performed miracles such as healing the sick, calming storms and aiding sailors, earning him veneration as a protector of Zakynthos. Bilocation is well-documented, with accounts of him seen helping sailors while his body remained in the church. Locals also claimed to see him assisting those in need far from his monastery. His tomb occasionally resists opening, which is believed to indicate he is away performing miracles.

St. John the Wonderworker (John Maximovitch, 1896–1966), also known as Saint John of Shanghai and San Francisco, often demonstrated bilocation, healing, and clairvoyance. Exhumed in 1994, his relics were intact, now at St. John's Cathedral in San Francisco. His body remains flexible and emits a faint fragrance, venerated as a sign of holiness. St. John practiced intense prayer, fasting, and asceticism, often sleeping little to serve the poor and sick. He performed many miracles, including healing a child of leukemia and foretelling events, with many posthumous healings reported at his shrine. Thus he is sometimes called St. John the Wonderworker. Bilocation was frequent, with accounts of him appearing in hospitals or churches while physically elsewhere, such as in Shanghai and San Francisco. His incorrupt relics continue to inspire devotion and reported miracles.

The miracles of **St. Alexander Svirsky** (1448–1533) are established in Russian literature because he healed the Tsars. His incorruptible body was perfectly preserved for 400+ years; it was rediscovered in 1998 at Alexander-Svirsky Monastery. The relics remain remarkably intact, with soft tissue and a sweet fragrance, despite centuries of exposure. St. Alexander practiced strict asceticism, including prolonged fasting, solitary prayer, and living in a wilderness hermitage. He was known for miracles like healing a paralyzed nobleman and receiving a vision of the Holy Trinity, a rare spiritual event. His relics continue to be a source of healing miracles for pilgrims.

THERAVADA BUDDHISM – SRI LANKA

In Sri Lanka, the phenomenon of incorruptible bodies is primarily associated with highly revered Theravada Buddhist monks said to have achieved the status of Arhats *(arahants)* or advanced meditators. Here are a few cases of individuals who engaged in a lot of spiritual cultivation practices, and whose remains show little to no decay, which in Buddhism is usually interpreted as a sign of high spiritual attainment:

After his death, the body of **Venerable Kadawedduwe Jinavamsa** (1907–1971) remained fresh for days without embalming, drawing thousands of devotees. His remains, preserved in a glass reliquary, show minimal decay and a lifelike appearance, and are venerated at Sri Lanka's

INCORRUPTIBLE BODIES AND BILOCATION MIRACLES

Kelaniya Raja Maha Vihara. He practiced vipassana meditation, fasting, and Dhamma teaching, and founded the Sri Kalyani Yogashrama Samstha to revive Theravada monasticism. Miracles attributed to him include healing the sick and guiding devotees through spiritual insights, with his preservation seen as evidence of Arhatship. His relics continue to inspire reverence, symbolizing his profound meditative attainment.

After his death, the body of **Venerable Kiribathgoda Gnanananda** (1921–2015) showed minimal decay for weeks, and was later cremated with the relics preserved. His remains, before cremation, retained a fresh appearance with soft skin, and were enshrined temporarily at Sri Lanka's Mahamevnawa Monastery, with crystalline *sharira* relics venerated post-cremation. When alive he practiced vipassana meditation, Dhamma preaching, asceticism, and founded the Mahamevnawa Buddhist Monastery to spread Theravada teachings. Miracles include reported healings and spiritual visions among devotees, with his incorruptible preservation linked to his meditative purity. His relics draw pilgrims, embodying his legacy of accessible Buddhist practice.

The body of **Venerable Wariyapola Sri Sumangala** (1795–1865) resisted decay; the relics are now kept at Wariyapola Temple. His remains, preserved in a glass case, show minimal decomposition with a lifelike quality, and are revered as a sign of Arhatship. He practiced vipassana meditation, fasting, and leadership in Theravada Buddhism, notably resisting colonial rule to protect Sri Lanka's Buddhist heritage. Miracles attributed to him include inspiring resistance movements and spiritual blessings, with his preservation considered a sign of Arhatship. His relics at Wariyapola Temple continue to attract devotees.

Venerable Matara Sri Nanarama (1901–1992) was a vipassana meditation master whose body decomposed unusually slowly, prompting reverence because incorruptibility in Buddhism is linked to enlightenment as a sign the practitioner had achieved Arhatship. His remains, preserved temporarily before cremation, showed minimal decay with a fresh appearance, with *sharira* relics (after cremation) venerated at Sri Lanka's Mitirigala Nissarana Vanaya. He practiced intensive vipassana meditation, asceticism, and Dhamma teaching, revitalizing insight meditation in Sri

Lanka. Miracles include guiding disciples to spiritual insights and reported healings near his relics. His relics continue to inspire meditation practitioners, reflecting his legacy of mindfulness teachings.

THERAVADA BUDDHISM – VIETNAM

In Vietnam, the "incorruptible body" of a saint, a well-recognized spiritual phenomenon associated with ardent cultivators, is called *Nhục thân bất hoại*.

Two recent cases include **Venerable Thích Thanh Quang** (20th century), whose body remains undecomposed at Chùa Đại Tòng Lâm (Bà Rịa-Vũng Tàu Province) decades after death due to a lifetime of meditation work. His remains, preserved in a glass reliquary, are remarkably intact with minimal decay and a faint fragrance, venerated as a sign of spiritual purity. He practiced intensive meditation, fasting, and Buddhist preaching, dedicating his life to teaching Vinaya and compassion. Miracles attributed to him include healing devotees and spiritual visions, with his preservation attributed to his meditative attainment.

The body of Senior Buddhist Patriarch **Venerable Thích Trí Tịnh** (1917–2014), though not fully incorruptible, showed minimal decay for weeks after passing, attributed to his lifelong asceticism. His remains, preserved in a reliquary at Vĩnh Nghiêm Pagoda (Ho Chi Minh City), retain a lifelike quality with slight deterioration, and are enhanced for veneration. He practiced Pure Land meditation, fasting, and scriptural translation, notably rendering key Buddhist texts into Vietnamese. Miracles attributed to him include spiritual guidance through dreams and reported healings among devotees.

THERAVADA BUDDHISM – LAOS

In Laos, the phenomenon of incorruptible bodies is primarily associated with Theravada Buddhist monks who are believed to have attained high levels of spiritual purity (*arahants* or advanced meditators). These cases are revered as sacred, and the preserved bodies are often enshrined in temples for veneration. Incorruptibility is seen as proof of deep *samadhi* attainments, which means the individual achieved some stage of Arhatship. Preserved bodies are enshrined as objects of devotion.

The body of the forest monk, **Phra Ajaan Khamphanh** (20th century), did not decay after death and was placed in a glass case at Wat Pa Ban Tat (Laos). His remains are remarkably preserved, with soft skin and minimal deterioration, emitting a faint fragrance considered a mark of sanctity. He practiced intensive *samadhi* meditation, asceticism, and Dhamma teaching in the Theravada forest tradition, living a secluded life in northern Laos. Miracles attributed to him include healing the sick and guiding devotees through spiritual visions, with his preservation seen as evidence of Arhatship. His relics draw devotees because they prove his deep meditative attainments.

Phra Ajaan Thet Thetrangsi (1902–1994), a student of the Thai master Ajaan Mun, showed little decay and was enshrined at Wat Hin Mak Peng (Nong Khai, Thailand near Lao border). His body, preserved in a glass reliquary, retains a lifelike appearance with minimal decomposition, often described as fragrant by devotees. He practiced vipassana meditation, asceticism, and Dhamma preaching; he led the Thai Forest Tradition in northeast Thailand. He was widely known for psychic powers, and miracles include reported healings and spiritual guidance, with his preservation linked to his meditative purity. Disciples reported seeing him cross rivers by walking on water when no boats were available. He occasionally vanished from one place and reappeared miles away, especially when helping devotees in emergencies. Many claimed to be cured of diseases after receiving his blessings or meditation instructions. He accurately foretold his own death, which is common for the saints of nearly all traditions, and the fates of some disciples. He spoke of encounters with devas and spirits, teaching that meditation purified the mind to perceive them. His teachings greatly influenced Theravada communities in Thailand and Laos.

THERAVADA BUDDHISM – BURMA

In Burma (Myanmar), the phenomenon of incorruptible bodies after death is deeply tied to Theravada Buddhism, where revered monks (*arahants* or advanced meditators) are believed to achieve bodily preservation through spiritual mastery. Below are notable Burmese monks whose bodies reportedly remained intact after death, often enshrined for veneration:

One of the most famous cases in Myanmar, the body of **Sayadaw U Narada** (1868–1955) shows minimal decay decades after death and are venerated as a sign of Arhatship. His undecomposed body is enshrined in a glass reliquary at Mingun Jetavana Monastery (near Mandalay). The remains retain soft tissue and a lifelike appearance, with a sweet fragrance reported by pilgrims. He practiced vipassana meditation, strict Vinaya adherence, and Dhamma teaching, revitalizing insight meditation in Burma as one of its key teachers. Miracles attributed to him include healing the sick, appearing in dreams to guide meditators, and the ability to read minds and predict disciples' spiritual progress, with his preservation considered a divine mark. He had a great influence across Myanmar's monastic communities. His relics currently draw thousands because they demonstrate a profound spiritual attainment.

Revered for his compassion and asceticism, pilgrims visit to pay respects to the remains of **Thamanya Sayadaw** (1913–2003). His body was not embalmed yet remained intact, now enshrined at Thamanya Monastery with its preservation linked to his Arhatship. The remains show minimal decay, with a lifelike quality and faint fragrance, and are preserved in a glass reliquary as a mark of sanctity. He practiced vipassana meditation, fasting, and charitable acts, founding a monastery to serve the poor in Karen State, Myanmar. Miracles include reported healings and protection of devotees during conflict. His relics continue to inspire devotion, reflecting his legacy of selflessness.

The body of **Webu Sayadaw** (1896–1977) was said to remain fresh for weeks before cremation, with some remains preserved since among his ashes were crystalline relics (*sariras*). These remains are venerated at Webu Sayadaw Monastery (Kyaukse, Myanmar), and give off a reported fragrance and radiant quality. He practiced *anapanasati* (mindfulness of breathing), strict asceticism, Dhamma teaching, and emphasized meditation for laypeople. Miracles include reported healings, spiritual awakenings among disciples, being sustained by devas, and his crystal-like *sariras* are considered a miraculous sign of enlightenment.

THERAVADA BUDDHISM – CAMBODIA

In Cambodia, the phenomenon of incorruptible bodies is deeply tied to Theravada Buddhism, where revered monks (*arahants* or advanced meditators) are believed to achieve bodily preservation through spiritual mastery. Below are notable Cambodian monks whose bodies have remained intact after death, and often enshrined for veneration:

Venerable Luong Por Ta Dang (early 20th Century). His undecomposed body is enshrined in a glass case at Wat Ta Dang (Battambang Province). Locals believe his body emits a fragrant scent (*divya gandha*), a mark of sanctity. His remains are remarkably preserved, with minimal decay and a lifelike appearance, venerated as a sign of spiritual mastery. He practiced *samadhi* meditation, asceticism, and Dhamma teaching, serving Cambodia's rural communities. Miracles include reported healings and spiritual guidance, with his fragrance and physical preservation linked to Arhatship. His relics draw devotees, embodying his legacy of compassion and meditation.

Venerable Preah Achariya Tieng (19th–20th Century) His body showed no decay for months after death; now preserved at Wat Nokor Bachey (Kampong Cham). Followers report healing blessings near his relics. His remains, preserved through lacquer, retain a lifelike quality with minimal deterioration, and are enshrined as a sacred relic. He practiced *samadhi* meditation, Vinaya discipline, and charitable acts, leading Theravada communities in Cambodia. His miracles include granting spiritual visions alongside healings, with his preservation considered a mark of enlightenment. His relics continue to inspire devotion, with ongoing healings reported.

Known for deep *samadhi* (meditative absorption) practices, the body of **Venerable Krouch Sam Ath** (20th century) remained lifelike for weeks before being lacquered and enshrined at Wat Sopheak Mongkol (Takeo). His remains, gilded and preserved, show minimal decay with a serene expression, and are venerated as a sign of Arhatship. He practiced intensive *samadhi* meditation, fasting, and Dhamma teaching, serving rural Cambodian communities. Miracles include healings and spiritual guidance, with his preservation understood as linked to his meditative purity.

THERAVADA BUDDHISM – THAILAND

The body of **Luang Pu Sodh Candasaro** (1884–1959), founder of the Dhammakaya tradition, though technically embalmed has remained lifelike for decades with minimal decay, his skin staying supple. His remains, enshrined at Wat Dhammakaya (Pathum Thani, Thailand), retain a remarkable appearance, with a faint fragrance noted by devotees. He practiced Dhammakaya (*dharmakaya*) meditation, asceticism, Dhamma teaching, and founded a global Buddhist movement. Miracles include reported healings and spiritual visions, with his preservation considered a sign of meditative mastery.

Koh Samui's mummified monk at Wat Khunaram, **Luang Pho Daeng** (1894-1973), died in in a seated meditative position, and ever since his body has been on display in an upright glass case at the temple. Almost fifty years since his death, his body shows little sign of decay, with minimal deterioration and a serene expression, preserved naturally without embalming. He practiced *samadhi* meditation, asceticism, and Dhamma teaching, living a simple life in southern Thailand. Miracles include reported spiritual guidance and protection for devotees, with his preservation seen as a mark of Arhatship. His presence draws thousands to Koh Samui where his relics inspire awe, and attest to his meditative attainments.

Famous for meditation powers, **Luang Phu Waen Sujinno's** (1887–1985) undecomposed body was covered in gold leaf and is seated in a glass reliquary at Wat Doi Mae Pang (Chiang Rai) where it remains visibly intact. His remains show minimal decay, with soft skin and a lifelike posture, emitting a faint fragrance revered as *divya gandha*. He practiced vipassana meditation, asceticism, and Dhamma teaching, wandering as a forest monk in northern Thailand. Miracles include healings and levitation during meditation, with his body's preservation linked to the attainment of Arhatship.

After the death of **Luang Por Koon Parisuttho** (1923–2015), his body showed no signs of decay for weeks despite no embalming. Later it was lacquered and gilded. One of Thailand's most beloved monks, his shrine at Wat Ban Rai (Nakhon Ratchasima) attracts millions. His remains retain a lifelike appearance with minimal deterioration, and are venerated because they are a sign of spiritual attainment. He practiced *samadhi* meditation, charitable acts, and Dhamma teaching, blessing millions with amulets and spiritual guidance. His miracles include reported healings and protection from accidents, with his preservation considered a sign of spiritual attainments.

Luang Phu Sim Buddhacaro (1909–1992) – his body remained flexible after death and is now preserved in a meditative posture under glass at Wat Tham Pha Plong (Chiang Dao, Thailand). His remains show minimal decay, with soft tissue and a serene expression, preserved naturally. He practiced vipassana meditation, asceticism, and Dhamma teaching, guiding disciples in the Thai Forest Tradition. Miracles include reported healings and spiritual insights, and devotees still report visions of him in their dreams.

VAJRAYANA BUDDHISM

The preserved body of **Dambo Lama Dashi-Dorzho Itigilov** (1852-1927), a famous Buryat Buddhist monk (from Russia's Buryatia region), remains one of Buddhism's most remarkable phenomena of bodily incorruption. Itigilov served as the head of Russian Buddhism from 1911 to 1917 and was known for his extraordinary spiritual practices, including advanced meditation techniques called *tukdam* (meditation on the clear light of death) and *phowa* (consciousness transference). He passed away while seated in the lotus position.

Before his death in 1927, Itigilov instructed his disciples to exhume his body after specific intervals – first after 30 years, then again in 75 years. His uncorrupted body was first exhumed in 1955 and found remarkably preserved, then reburied until its final exhumation in 2002, when Russian forensic scientists confirmed the complete absence of any embalming procedures. The body, sitting in perfect lotus posture, displays lifelike skin elasticity, intact hair and nails, and minimal weight loss, suggesting an unprecedented state of post-mortem preservation directly attributed to his mastery of Tibetan Buddhist death meditation practices. The scientists present reported that his body was in the condition of someone who had died only 36 hours prior.

Today, his body is housed in a climate-controlled glass shrine at Ivolginsky Datsan monastery near Ulan-Ude, Buryatia where it attracts thousands of pilgrims who consider him a "living Buddha" and report miraculous healings and spiritual experiences in his presence.

The uncorrupted remains of **Bogd Khan VIII** (Jebtsundamba Khutuktu, 1869–1924), the eighth Bogd Khan of Mongolia and head of Mongolian Buddhism, were initially preserved at Gandan Monastery in Ulaanbaatar, where his body was kept in a golden stupa following his death. Unlike Itigilov, Bogd Khan VIII's preservation appears to have involved partial mummification techniques combined with Tibetan Buddhist mortuary practices, including the application of sacred herbs. Historical accounts describe his body as remarkably preserved, sitting in meditation posture with lifelike features and continuing to grow hair and nails for years after death.

The Bogd Khan was renowned for his extensive spiritual practices, including decades-long retreats in mountain caves, mastery of *tummo* (inner heat) meditation that allowed him to survive Mongolian winters in thin clothing, and his claimed ability to remain in *samadhi* (deep meditative absorption) for weeks at a time. Tragically, his sacred remains became a target during Stalin's anti-religious campaigns of the 1930s, when Soviet authorities systematically destroyed Buddhist monasteries throughout Mongolia and Buryatia.

The Bogd Khan's body was secretly removed from Gandan in 1937 and burned along with thousands of other religious artifacts, ending what monks had maintained as a century-long tradition of preserving the incorruptible bodies of high lamas through a combination of spiritual practice and traditional preservation methods.

The body of **Terton Sogyal Lerab Lingpa** (1856–1926), a terton (treasure revealer) linked to Padmasambhava's prophecies, is located at Dzogchen Monastery, Kham. His body remained lifelike for weeks after death, with no decay, before being enshrined in a stupa. His remains, preserved in a stupa, reportedly retained soft skin and a faint fragrance, with devotees noting a radiant quality as a sign of his spiritual mastery. Terton Sogyal practiced intensive Dzogchen meditation, tantric rituals, and retreats in sacred caves, revealing *terma* (hidden teachings) such as the Tendrel Nyesel and Vajrakilaya cycles. He was renowned for miracles, including prophesying future events and revealing treasures like the Yang Nying Pudri cycle, with his spiritual connection to Padmasambhava evident in visions. His relics at Dzogchen Monastery continue to inspire devotion, symbolizing his role as a bridge to Padmasambhava's teachings.

The body of **Dudjom Lingpa** (1835–1904), a Dzogchen visionary, showed no decay after death. His remains, enshrined in a stupa, are described as remarkably intact with a glowing quality, with *sharira* (crystalline relics) reportedly emitting light, and are venerated as a mark of Arhatship. Dudjom Lingpa practiced Dzogchen meditation, solitary retreats, and tantric rituals, receiving direct visions from deities and masters like Guru Rinpoche, which informed his *terma* revelations. He performed miracles, including predicting his reincarnation as **Dudjom Rinpoche** (1904-1987) and revealing profound teachings like the Dudjom Tersar, with disciples witnessing his ability to manipulate weather. His relics continue to draw pilgrims, embodying his legacy as a Dzogchen visionary.

The body of **Shabkar Tsokdruk Rangdrol** (1781–1851), hermit yogi, are now enshrined at Amnye Machen Mountain, Tibet. His body remained fresh for months in a meditative posture (*tukdam*) before being enshrined. His remains, preserved in a stupa, reportedly retained a lifelike appearance with minimal decay, with devotees noting a sweet fragrance as a sign of his yogic attainment. Shabkar practiced Dzogchen meditation, solitary retreats in caves, and nonsectarian teachings, composing poetic songs like those in his Flight of the Garuda to guide disciples. He was known for miracles, including taming wild animals and granting spiritual insights, with his vegetarian advocacy reflecting his compassion.

MAHAYANA BUDDHISM – CHINA

The uncorrupted body of the Sixth Patriarch of Chan (Zen) Buddhism, **Hui Neng** (638–713), is on display at Nanhua Temple, Guangdong. His lacquered body has been seated in meditation for 1,300+ years, with minimal decay, retaining a lifelike appearance and soft texture, enhanced by gold leaf. Hui Neng practiced Chan meditation, simplicity, and scriptural teaching, famously achieving sudden enlightenment upon hearing the *Diamond Sutra*. His profound teachings transformed Chan Buddhism and there are reported visions of his presence guiding disciples. His teachings shaped the Southern Chan school. His relics, alongside those of Hanshan Deqing, continue to draw devotees.

The body of the Ming Dynasty monk, **Master Hanshan Deqing** (1546–1623), is also located at Nanhua Temple alongside Master Hui Neng's body. His mummified remains, preserved through lacquer and gold leaf, show minimal decay with intact features, enshrined as a testament to his spiritual reforms. Hanshan practiced intensive Chan meditation, fasting, and scriptural study, leading large-scale renovations at Nanhua Temple to revive Chan Buddhism. His miracles include visions of divine beings and guiding devotees through teachings, with his preservation considered a sign of enlightenment. His influence as a reformer extended across Ming China. His relics at Nanhua Temple continue to inspire pilgrims.

China calls incorruptible bodies "whole body relics" and as you can see, a number of temples contain the incorruptible bodies of past Chinese Buddhist monks. In particular, a number of temples on Jiuhua Mountain preserve the whole body relics of past spiritual masters:

- Dabei Temple – Monk Cihang
- Zhantanlin Temple – Monk Mingjing
- Tiantai Temple – Monk Puhui

Monk Cihang's (1893–1954) body at Dabei Temple is preserved through lacquer and gold leaf, maintaining a lifelike appearance with minimal natural decay, and is revered as a sign of his spiritual mastery. He practiced Chan meditation, fasting, and compassionate service, teaching Buddhism in China and Taiwan, where he founded the Buddhist Association of Taiwan. Miracles attributed to him include healing devotees and guiding lost travelers, with his posthumous preservation considered a testament to his attainment. His gilded relics draw pilgrims to Jiuhua Mountain.

Monk Mingjing's (1879–1948) body at Zhantanlin Temple is mummified with lacquer, showing remarkable preservation and a serene expression, enshrined as a sacred relic. He practiced rigorous Chan meditation, asceticism, and scriptural recitation, living a secluded life dedicated to spiritual cultivation. His miracles include reported healings and visions experienced by devotees near his relics, with his preservation linked to his meditative purity.

Monk Puhui's (1888–1957) body at Tiantai Temple is preserved through lacquer, retaining intact features and a meditative posture, venerated as a sign of enlightenment. He practiced intensive meditation, fasting, and devotion to Ksitigarbha Bodhisattva, serving as a revered teacher on Jiuhua Mountain. Miracles attributed to him include protecting devotees from harm and granting spiritual insights, with his relics believed to emit a faint fragrance.

At Zhenru Temple in Jiangxi Province rests the incorruptible body remains of **Master Hsu Yun** (1840–1959), a highly revered modern Chan master whose body was preserved after death. His remains, found intact upon exhumation, are described as remarkably preserved with soft tissue and a faint fragrance, and enshrined as a testament to his spiritual attainment. Master Hsu Yun practiced rigorous Chan meditation, fasting, and pilgrimage, often walking thousands of miles (enduring extreme hardships) to holy sites like Mount Putuo. He was known for miracles, including surviving a severe beating at age 112 and healing devotees through his presence, with his *sariras* (relics) emitting a five-colored light after cremation. Accounts of bilocation are rare, but his spiritual influence was felt across China, with disciples reporting his guidance in distant locations. His relics at Zhenru Temple continue to inspire pilgrims, symbolizing his profound Chan mastery.

At Yunju Temple in Beijing sits the body of **Master Haihui** (16th century), a Ming Dynasty monk whose mummified body is enshrined there. His remains, preserved through natural mummification, show minimal decay with intact skin and features, and are venerated as a sign of spiritual purity. Master Haihui practiced intense Chan meditation, asceticism, and scriptural study, dedicating his life to monastic discipline at Yunju Temple. While specific miracles are less documented, his preservation is considered a miraculous testament to his meditative attainment, with devotees reporting spiritual blessings near his relics.

The body of **Master Yixing** (683–727), a Tang Dynasty monk and astronomer, is found at Guoqing Temple in Zhejiang Province. His remains, preserved through mummification, are remarkably intact with minimal decay, enshrined as a sacred relic attesting to his spiritual mastery. Master Yixing practiced Buddhist meditation, scriptural study, and asceticism, integrating his astronomical expertise with spiritual discipline, notably developing the Chinese calendar under Emperor Xuanzong. He was renowned for intellectual accomplishments, such as precise astronomical predictions and contributions to Tang Dynasty science, though no supernatural feats are widely recorded. His relics at Guoqing Temple still attract devotees today.

MAHAYANA BUDDHISM – KOREA

In Korean Buddhism, there have been rare cases where the entire body resists decomposition, which is more common in China due to Korea's humidity.

One documented case is that of **Venerable Cheongdam** (1898–1994) – a female meditation master who practiced at Naewonsa Temple (South Jeolla Province). Her body remained fresh and supple for forty days without embalming, with a faint fragrance reported, and her cremation yielded numerous pearl-like *sariras*, venerated as a sign of Arhatship.

Venerable Cheongdam practiced intensive Seon (Zen) meditation, strict Vinaya adherence, and asceticism, likely participating in the three-month summer and winter meditation retreats typical of Korean Buddhist nuns. She was known for miracles, including spiritual guidance that inspired profound transformations among disciples, though specific miracles are less documented due to her humility and the rarity of female monastics in historical records. Her *sarira* relics at Naewonsa Temple continue to draw pilgrims, and prove that a female master can also purify their body enough to produce this phenomenon.

HINDUISM, TAOISM, TANTRA AND OTHER TRADITIONS

INCORRUPTIBLE BODIES AND BILOCATION MIRACLES

Jewish burial laws and Kohanim restrictions discourage exhumation, making incorruptibility claims rare or unverified because of strict prohibitions against disturbing graves. Nonetheless, Rabbi Louis Ginzberg's *Legends of the Jews* mentions an alleged case of incorruptibility for **Baruch**, Jeremiah's scribe, whose tomb in Iraq was said to be preserved, his body remained uncorrupted in the tomb, and his scrolls and writing instruments were preserved beside him. However, this is based on Jewish Apocrypha and Aggadah, lacking historical verification, and no modern exhumation confirms it. It may simply be a story symbolizing the eternity of Torah wisdom because as Jeremiah's scribe, Baruch recorded divine prophecy. Even so, many Jews – especially devoted rabbis – have no doubt achieved incorruptible bodies due to their spiritual practice but we simply have not discovered them yet.

Taoist teachings emphasize achieving the stage of an immortal (Arhat or *xian*) through internal alchemy (*neijia* inner energy exercises) that will purify the body's vital energy enough so that the inner subtle body can become differentiated from its shell and all other body energies with distinctness. Because it becomes distinctly differentiated from its physical container due to becoming separated out because of a higher grade of purity, it can become free of the human shell pre-death, thus making one a spiritual master through the first or second *dhyana* attainment.

Though the cases have not been verified, the Taoists said to have exhibited incorruptible bodies include **Master Huang Yuanji** (late 18th to 19th century), a Qing dynasty Taoist master of the Dragon Gate (Longmen) sect whose body was said to have remained incorrupt and enshrined on Qingcheng Mountain in Sichuan, China. Later it was buried, but relics of his hair and nails were preserved.

Master Li Hanxu (early 19th century), a Qing dynasty Taoist who practiced *neidan* (inner alchemy), is also said to have achieved a saintly death without decay. Records are unclear whether his body was enshrined on Mount Emei or not. Li Hanxu claimed to have received teachings from the legendary Zhang Sanfeng (14th-century immortal) in a dream or meditative vision. This inspired him to synthesize *Neidan* (Inner Alchemy) practices from multiple traditions, which he formulated into three stages: "Laying the Foundation" by purifying the body through diet, breathing, and ethical living; "Circulating the Light" by visualizing energy flowing in the body's Qi meridians and elsewhere; and "Forming the Golden Elixir," which meant purifying one's Yin and Yang energies to achieve spiritual immortality. Alongside **Master Wu Chongxu**, Li Hanxu formalized the Western School of Taoist Alchemy, distinct from the Northern (Quanzhen) and Southern (Zhengyi) schools.

There should be far more instances of Taoists who achieved physical incorruptibility because they succeeded in attaining the higher bodies, but such are unconfirmed and no physical evidence exists today primarily because most Taoist bodies are cremated.

Many Indonesian Muslims venerate tombs of saints (*wali*) believed to have incorruptible bodies, such as the Islamic saint **Sunan Gunung Jati** (1448–1568), one of the Wali Songo (Nine Saints) who spread Islam in Java. Locals claim his body remains intact within his tomb at Astana Gunung Jati, but this is unverified. Across the world many shrines have been built for Islamic saints, known for lives of holiness and miraculous powers, whose remains still rest therein, but until they are opened we cannot verify incorruptibility or not.

For Hinduism, we are a little luckier in finding two modern confirmed cases of the initial phase of incorruptibility. The first is that of **Swami Sivananda** (1887–1963), a yoga master known for bilocation and the miracle of healing through touch, whose body remained fresh for days before cremation (Rishikesh). His remains, observed by devotees at the Divine Life Society, showed no signs of decay for several days, retaining a lifelike appearance and emitting a faint fragrance, considered a mark of his spiritual attainment.

Swami Sivananda practiced intense Kriya Yoga, Vedantic meditation, and daily scriptural study, authoring over 200 books to spread Hindu philosophy globally. He was renowned for miracles, including healing chronic illnesses through touch and guiding disciples spiritually. His ashram in Rishikesh became a hub for such events. Bilocation was well-documented, with credible reports of him appearing to devotees in distant locations, such as during meditation sessions in India and abroad, while physically remaining in Rishikesh. His legacy endures through the Divine

Life Society, with his cremated relics venerated as a source of spiritual inspiration.

The body of **Paramahansa Yogananda** (1893–1952), Kriya Yoga Guru and famous author of *Autobiography of a Yogi*, also showed no decay for over thirty days after death. Harry T. Rowe, the Mortuary Director of Forest Lawn Memorial-Park Association, wrote a notarized letter wherein he stated that Yogananda's body showed no signs of decay for three weeks after his death, a phenomenon he described as "an unparalleled one" and "the most extraordinary case" they had encountered. In addition to remaining in a state of immutability, the letter also mentioned that no odor of decay was present at any time, further supporting the claim of the body's preservation.

Yogananda practiced Kriya Yoga meditation, pranayama (breath control), and daily devotion to God, teaching self-realization through the Self-Realization Fellowship, which he founded in 1920. He was known for miracles, including healing devotees of physical ailments and demonstrating clairvoyance, with accounts of his presence calming turbulent seas during voyages. Bilocation was frequently reported, with disciples witnessing him in multiple locations simultaneously, such as appearing in India while physically in California, as noted in *Autobiography of a Yogi*.

In Nepal, the mummified body of **Siddha Guru Bamdev** (11th–12th Century), a tantric yogi who is a legendary figure in both Hindu and Buddhist tantra, is enshrined at Bamdev Temple; devotees claim it emits healing energy. His mummified remains, preserved through natural or ritual processes, are reported to show minimal decay, with devotees noting a radiant quality and subtle fragrance as signs of spiritual purity. Bamdev practiced intensive tantric sadhana, including meditation, mantra recitation, and yogic austerities, likely in cremation grounds, aligning with the Mahasiddha tradition of mastering siddhis (spiritual powers). Miracles attributed to him include healing ailments and granting spiritual insights, with his temple's energy believed to cure devotees, though specific historical accounts are scarce. His relics at Bamdev Temple continue to draw pilgrims, embodying his legacy as a bridge between Hindu and Buddhist tantric traditions.

THE KUNDALINI PURIFICATION PROCESS

In the Christianity, incorruptibility is considered a sign of saintliness. In the eastern traditions – such as Buddhism, Taoism and Hinduism – incorruptibility is seen as proof of meditative accomplishment, namely the spiritual attainment of Arhatship (enlightenment) achieved by attaining the higher spiritual bodies.

Across the world, whether in the east or west, the whole body relics of incorruptible bodies inspire devotion among followers who often visit them to beseech these accomplished saints for aid. This is because the transcendental spiritual bodies of an attainee grant him a degree of longevity (so people know he still lives) as well as miraculous powers of intercession through his higher bodies.

The major reason we don't find more cases of incorruption is simply because most monks in the eastern traditions are cremated, whereupon their followers often find *sarira* crystal or pearl-like relics that they then venerate after the whole body is burned. Sometimes these rocklike relics, when isolated in glass cases, actually give birth to even more relics like themselves.

In some spiritual traditions, exhumation is not allowed so uncorrupted bodies may exist but will always remain undiscovered. And in some cases, a country may be so humid that corruption can last only for a short while until the deteriorating powers of the weather destroy it. It is easiest to achieve the ranks of the spiritual path in arid, dry or temperate climates, and bodies last longer under such conditions, too.

You must go through a lengthy, multi-year process of Prana purification that cleanses your physical body to make the subtle body achievement possible. This lengthy purification process is what produces the uncorrupted physical body remains after death. Individuals always confuse the movement of inner Prana with either their own spiritual energies (kundalini, Qi, Prana, etc.) or the energies of the Holy Spirit, God and so forth when they are actually due to the intercession of higher spiritual masters. As stated, those energies, coursing through your body continuously for years, consequently produce incorruptibility.

CHAPTER 4:
THE YIN-YANG EMOTIONAL UPHEAVAL OF KUNDALINI PURIFICATION

To save time, let us use eastern terms and refer to this spiritual purification process as "kundalini purification," and let us use the terms "Qi" and "Prana" interchangeably to denote the life force, vital energy, or subtle energy of our body. After being continuously cleansed by spiritual kundalini energies that are the life force of higher-bodied beings, your transformed physical body can survive for years before showing signs of decay. How long the incorruptibility lasts depends upon the spiritual procedures used in the purification process, how long the individual practiced, as well as the weather and environmental conditions that the body was exposed to after death.

In both Hinduism and Buddhism, practitioners are guided by spiritual teachings that describe the stages and sensations of kundalini transformation – a profound process of Prana (life force) purification. This journey is not undertaken alone; it is said to require the support and intervention of many spiritual masters, saints, and sages who lend you their purifying energies to take you through it. A key principle in these traditions is that the unusual internal energy movements or sensations one experiences are not self-generated, but rather the result of external spiritual assistance working within you to accelerate your evolution.

Hindu tradition offers a symbolic explanation of the process through the myth of the Churning of the Ocean of Milk, where the ocean represents the body's Prana. In the story, devas and asuras – divine forces and shadow forces like the duality of Yin and Yang – cooperate in churning the ocean to extract *amrita*, the nectar of immortality, which represents the higher immortal spiritual bodies. This cosmic stirring represents the intense inner friction of the kundalini process as the energy revolves around inside you. Just as heat arises from physical friction, the burning heat often felt during kundalini awakening *partly* stems from the energetic friction produced within the body, as higher spiritual energy stirs and purifies dormant or impure layers of your Prana through frictional contact, and part of the heat is due to the fact that *warm Yang energy* is involved. This inner fire is a hallmark of transformation – painful at times, but essential for the birth of a refined, subtle spiritual body.

Because kundalini awakening can ultimately result in the separation of the subtle body from the physical body, it is often referred to as the "fire of separation" in many Yoga traditions. This process is not always accompanied by heat, however; at times, the body may become unusually cold as its Yin energies are flooded and cleansed by external purifying Yin forces. These forces typically come from enlightened spiritual masters who are moving your energies with their own. If you are an Arhat or Great Golden Arhat, you possess the ability to move, adjust, and even transform the quality and temperature of *nirmanakaya* energy that you can overlay upon a practitioner's body. This compassionate assistance is vital, and such help usually only occurs for virtuous individuals who engage in serious spiritual disciplines – prayer, mantra, meditation, breathwork and so on. A true kundalini awakening is considered a rare grace, generally reserved for true saints and advanced spiritual aspirants.

A being who has attained a Supra-Causal or Superconsciousness body – such as a Great Arhat or Great Golden Arhat – can generate complex kundalini phenomena within any human body it enters. These include inner vibrations, waves of heat or cold, and other energy movements commonly mistaken for one's own internal Prana or "awakening energy." As stated, such sensations are often the result of *nirmanakaya* emanations – subtle bodies projected by exalted spiritual masters – working within you. They are *not* your own energies, which recipients quickly discover.

When you meditate or pray and consequently feel strange, inexplicable fluctuations of hot or cold energy, these are rarely self-generated and are not usually the Holy Spirit or God directly acting, but rather the intervention of compassionate masters who are assisting you with their own energy fields. They are the *grace* of other people's efforts to help you complete a very long process of purification so that you might ascend. The process is so troublesome and lengthy that only the saintly can earn this assistance over the many years required to differentiate the higher bodies out of the intermixed energy layers within us, which involves purifying the physical body enough so that it becomes incorruptible.

Hence, the help is not arbitrary. It comes as part of a long and difficult process of purification that few ever qualify for – and even then, only through great spiritual merit. The reason these masters aid you is not only altruism; your body becomes a training ground for their own disciples whom they bring with them when it is their turn to wash your energy. As they rotate energy throughout your body, they rotate the energy of their students' bodies as well using multiple *nirmanakaya* emanations for the audience, which stations in your brain. Your transformation becomes a group classroom – a rare local event that can benefit hundreds of subtle beings (devas) in the area, and others who pass in and out of you as each new spiritual master brings in their own students who are also practicing for ascension.

This cooperative effort explains why many saints, especially those sensitive to these energies, reported hearing laughter, voices, or chaotic clamor inside their heads during deep spiritual practice. These were not hallucinations, nor attacks by demonic forces as sometimes feared, but the energetic presence of spiritual masters and their deva disciples – beings temporarily entering your body to share in the purification work taking place.

Again, what happens is that while your body is being washed, the bodies of countless devas in the neighborhood who are qualified for ascension will also be washed as well, and they will also be using you to test their skills at affecting human consciousness. No one is going to work on you for years unless they also help their own students during that time, so hundreds of masters will rotate in and out of your body, taking their deva students with them, who will also receive the blessings of the purification efforts that use you as the base. The process is so troublesome and lengthy that only the saintly can earn this assistance, and now you can understand why they bother to do this work for people at all.

Buddhism describes eight common physical sensations frequently experienced by spiritual practitioners as kundalini energy begins to intensify and move throughout the body during this process. These sensations include: pain, itching, coldness, warmth, weightlessness, heaviness, roughness, and smoothness. These are considered normal signs of the body's energetic transformation, often marking the beginning of deeper inner purification.

An even longer list of possible sensations includes feelings of cold or coolness, heat or warmth, lightness, heaviness, roughness or coarseness, dryness, slipperiness, granular feelings, hardness, softness, tenderness, weakness, hurriedness or urgency, a feeling of being internally stuck, internal movements, itchiness, energeticness, slowness, soreness, aching or pain, swollenness, numbness, fullness, feelings of floating or sinking or being solid, feelings of being tired or rested, feelings of being sick or lost or drained, and the feeling of being courageous, scattered, dreamy, peaceful or quiet, old or dead, and hungry or thirsty.

From Buddhist sources, such as the *Surangama Sutra*, Eastern practitioners are also taught to expect a wide range of inner visions and perceptual phenomena when they begin to strongly cultivate spiritual practices. These may include seeing visions of things inside their body; observing an etheric shapeshifting transformation of saints or spiritual masters (that is an illusion); witnessing light radiating from objects or living beings; hearing celestial music, voices or conversations in the mind; and glimpsing extraordinary visions of distant lands, deities, or luminous realms (that are fake visions).

Practitioners may even find themselves able to see in darkness or perceive events occurring far away. The Chinese Buddhist monk Han Shan reported in his autobiography that he was able to temporarily see through walls and observe things at a distance, and so did **St. Porphyrios of Kavsokalyvia** (1906–1991), a revered elder of the Greek Orthodox Church, who once described seeing his fellow monks returning from a journey while they were still far off in the distance. When he revealed this vision to his elder, Father Panteleimon, Porphyrios was advised to keep such gifts private and use them with great caution. Saint Porphyrios said that he became able to see through water and rock formations to discover petroleum deposits, buried monuments, subterranean springs, and more.

While many of these experiences are part of the spiritual path, Buddhist teachings caution that most such visions are illusions – tests of attachment, not confirmations of attainment.

YIN & YANG PRANA – THE DUAL ENERGIES OF LIFE AND TRANSFORMATION

The most essential principle to understand about this churning purification process concerns the Yin and Yang, feminine and masculine, or negative and positive energies that animate all life. In Hinduism, yoga, Ayurveda and Indian martial arts, the body's life force is typically divided into five types of Prana – five *vayus* or energetic "winds." However, the *Brihadaranyaka Upanishad* offers an even more foundational insight, describing how the universe originally split itself into male and female – a symbolic division that maps directly onto the concept of Yin and Yang.

These two energies are recognized across the world's spiritual traditions, and are typically represented by the sun and moon, fire and water, or light and darkness. Yin is often associated with feminine, receptive, cool, and lunar qualities, while Yang embodies masculine, active, warm, and solar qualities. Yang energy feels like the warming rays of the sun, whereas Yin resembles the cooling glow of the moon. Therefore, you can expect Yang energies to be warm or hot, and Yin energies to be cool or even cold.

These polarities explain the temperature fluctuations – intense heat or warmth, icy coldness or just coolness – that practitioners often experience during the rotation of Prana within them. Such sensations are not random but directly related to the purification of the two primary Yin or Yang energetic currents flowing throughout the human body.

Religions such as Hinduism, Buddhism, and Taoism and their yogic or tantric offshoots, along with many other traditions, recognize this Yin-Yang framework under various names: positive-negative, sun-moon, male-female, solar-lunar. They all state that the human body is an alchemical vessel composed of both types of Prana, and both types of energy must be *refined (purified) and harmonized* over time through spiritual discipline.

Even in Christianity, this duality finds poetic expression. **St. Francis of Assisi**, in his *Canticle of Brother Sun and Sister Moon*, paid homage to these two fundamental types of Prana within the human body in a veiled sort of way. He wanted people to know why they feel hot and cold energies during the spiritual transformation process.

A valuable insight related to this topic comes from the widely circulated Finnish "heatmap" studies that visually represent how various emotions are felt in different parts of the human body. These maps – easily found online – illustrate that each emotion triggers unique patterns of energy activation, or Prana excitation, within the human body. In essence, a strong emotion changes the tone, quality, or "flavor" of your internal energy, creating *distinct sensations in specific body regions*. Each human emotion excites your Prana (internal energy) in a different sort of way by changing the place and way you feel it.

One notable study, titled "Bodily Maps of Emotions" by Lauri Nummenmaa, Enrico Glerean, Riitta Hari, and Jari Hietanen, systematically charted these patterns. Their research shows that emotions like anger, fear, love, or sadness produce different sensations felt in different areas of your body, reinforcing the idea that the mental-emotional events and body responses are deeply interconnected. To put it another way, a strong emotion changes the quality, temperament, quality or flavor of your Prana, and you will feel each emotion strongest at unique locations within your body.

These findings are more than just scientific curiosities – they form the foundation of many spiritual cultivation techniques found in both Eastern and Western traditions. In spiritual practice, emotions are often intentionally aroused to strongly (but temporarily) amplify, elevate or raise the corresponding type of Yin or Yang Qi connected with that emotion. Because different emotions (or "dominant attitudes") evoke different energetic responses within you, they serve as a way to uniquely differentiate your Yin Prana and Yang Prana from each other, which are typically intermixed in an undifferentiated fashion in individuals who do not spiritually cultivate. If you raise your Qi by spiking relevant emotions, and then cleanse that heightened Prana by frictional revolutions of Qi energy, this process over time will gradually purify your Prana and ultimately prepare the way for the emergence of a purified subtle body. This is the secret basis of the kundalini purification process emphasized in Yoga and Tantra.

Thermal imaging studies of the human body also reveal a big temperature drop in the hip region extending down through the legs, which is why this region undergoes a lot of Yin purification work during the later kundalini purification years. At that time, spiritual practitioners will often feel their legs being washed with very cold energies like ice, or their limbs will simply get very cold and stay that way without any special sensations of energy movement.

We've already seen several Christian saints complain about this phenomenon. Another notable example comes from the Zen master Hakuin, who reported that before he met his teacher Hakuyu he had practiced meditation so fiercely that his ears constantly heard a rushing sound, his lungs felt they were on fire and his legs felt as cold as ice, which were all due to the kundalini process unfolding.

To help him, his mountain teacher, Master Hakuyu, taught him a simple yet powerful visualization technique that anyone can use. He instructed Hakuin to visualize an egg of soft butter melting at the crown of the head, then slowly dripping down through his body, harmonizing the flow of energy and soothing internal imbalances. This gentle practice, rooted in internal energy medicine (*neidan* or *neijia*), remains a valuable tool for rebalancing your Qi/Prana that becomes uncomfortable due to spiritual practices. Master Hakuyu explained to Hakuin:

> Your condition is pitiable. By contemplating on truth too strenuously, you have lost the rhythm of spiritual advance, and that has finally brought on a grievous malady. And it is something very hard to cure, this Zen illness of yours [caused by over-exerted spiritual practices]. Though the sages of medicine frown over your case and put forth all their skill with needle and cautery and drugs, yet would they be helpless. ...
>
> From the mounting of the heart-fire your grievous illness has arisen. If you do not take it down you will never recover, though you learn and practice all the healing remedies human and divine. Now it may be that as my outward appearance is that of a Taoist, you fancy that my teaching is far from Buddhism. But this is Zen. One day, when you break through, you will see how laughable were your former ideas.
>
> This contemplation attains right contemplation by no-contemplation. Many-pointed contemplation is wrong contemplation. Hitherto your contemplation has been many-pointed and so you have contracted this grave malady. Is it not then proper to cure it by no-contemplation? If you now control the fire of heart and will and put it in the Tanden [*dan-tian*] and right down to the soles of the feet, your breast will of itself

become cool, without a thought of calculation, without a ripple of passion. This is true contemplation, pure contemplation. Do not call it dropping your Zen contemplation, for the Buddha himself says: "Hold your heart [mind] down in the soles of the feet and you heal a hundred and one ills." Further the Agama scriptures speak of the use of the So cream in curing mental exhaustion. The Tendai [Tien-tai school] meditation classic called "Stopping and Contemplation" deals in detail with illnesses and their causes, and describes the methods of treatment. It gives twelve different ways of breathing to cure various forms of illness, and it prescribes the method of visualizing a bean at the navel. The main point is always that the heart-fire must be taken down and kept at the Tanden and down to the soles, and this not only cures illness but very much helps Zen contemplation. ...

If the student finds in his meditation that the four great elements are out of harmony, and body and mind are fatigued, he should rouse himself and make this meditation. Let him visualize placed on the crown of his head that celestial So ointment, about as much as a duck's egg, pure in color and fragrance. Let him feel its exquisite essence and flavor melting and filtering down through his head, its flow permeating downwards, slowly laving the shoulders and elbows, the sides of the breast and within the chest, the lungs, liver, stomach and internal organs, the back and spine and hip bones. All the old ailments and adhesions and pains in the five organs and six auxiliaries follow the mind downwards. There is a sound as of the trickling of water. Percolating through the whole body, the flow goes gently down the legs, stopping at the soles of the feet.

Then let him make this meditation: that the elixir having permeated and filtered down through him, its abundance fills up the lower half of his body. It becomes warm, and he is saturated in it. Just as a skillful physician collects herbs of rare fragrance and puts them in a pan to boil, so the student feels that from the navel down he is simmering in the So elixir. When this meditation is being done there will be psychological experiences, of a sudden indescribable fragrance at the nose-tip, of a gentle and exquisite sensation in the body. Mind and body become harmonized and far surpass their condition at the peak of youth. Adhesions and obstructions are cleared away, the organs are tranquilized and insensibly the skin begins to glow. If the practice is carried on without relapse, what illness will not be healed, what power will not be acquired, what perfection will not be attained, what Way will not be fulfilled? The arrival of the result depends only on how the student performs the practices.[8]

It is especially important for spiritual practitioners to focus on activating and opening the lower regions of their body – from the pelvis down to the feet, including your genitals – through regular exercise and conscious inner energy work. Taoists provide spiritual inner washing methods for the breasts and genitals. You also need to focus on rotating the energy within your hands and fingers since the thermal heat map pictures show that these regions also suffer from reduced blood flow and poor circulation. Therefore they are also *major Prana circulation bottlenecks*. The Qi purification of the hands, feet, frontal face and genitalia is usually not performed as completely as for other areas of the body during the kundalini purification process.

Accordingly, it has been often noticed that the skin on the hands of partially incorrupt Christian saints resists decomposition, appears leathery and dehydrated, but are not rotting. As the thermal and Qi circulation maps suggest, if Prana has not been sufficiently refined in a particular area, that region is more prone to decomposition after death. Consequently, to prevent the hands from getting overlooked, Vajrayana (Tantric) Buddhists of Tibet always engage in performing special hand mudras so that their Qi washes the fingers and hands more thoroughly during the long kundalini purification process. Areas that undergo deeper spiritual and energetic cleansing are more likely to resist decay, reflecting the intimate link between Qi purification and physical preservation.

A profound psychological battle unfolds during the kundalini purification process as well, one that many spiritual practitioners are not prepared for. Buddhists familiar with the *Surangama Sutra* understand that they will be deliberately exposed to intense emotional states specifically designed to stimulate either Yin or Yang Prana in order to help purify these

---

[8] *The Tiger's Cave and Translations of Other Zen Writings*, Trevor Leggett, (Charles E. Tuttle, Rutland: Vermont, 1995), pp. 144-154.

energies within the body.

In this process, devas and their teachers use a *siddhi* power known as *anima* to shrink their form and assemble in the practitioner's brain around the brainstem, called the "pulpit," where a master will show them how the processes of thinking and feeling are generated within anatomy via Prana/Qi since it is basically a mechanism. There, under the guidance of an enlightened master, deva students will observe how consciousness operates as your brain fires with pranic energy during thought formation, or when someone creates, stores and retrieves memories from their neurons.

Under their teacher's supervision who is meanwhile rotating your Qi, these deva students will practice finding specific memories and implanting thoughts and emotions that trigger specific Yin or Yang emotional responses, such as guilt (Yin) or sexual desire (Yang). For example, they may provoke feelings of guilt (Yin) or desire (Yang) as demonstrations of their ability to influence human consciousness. In many cases they will simply show that they can block your thoughts so that you cannot remember some information.

To the uninformed practitioner, these experiences often feel like a psychic attack or oppression, leading them to believe they are under assault by devils or demons. But in reality, the individual is being used as a living classroom while their Prana is being purified – a training ground where divine beings are learning how to form thoughts in human minds in order to learn how to help people because all the work cannot be done by enlightened beings alone.

In everyday life, heavenly beings assist humanity by giving them helpful thoughts, but they must be trained how to do so. A person undergoing kundalini purification becomes a vessel for this training, which explains the psychological tension, mental pressure, and emotional turbulence often reported during the process.

The key to inner peace is learning to let go of the illusion that these thoughts are your own, and to watch the process with detachment as you might watch a waterfall, or the crashing of ocean waves on the surf that then disappear until new waves come in. Once you let go and simply observe the shenanigans by realizing that you aren't the one doing the thinking, then through detachment the agony of the process decreases.

PHYSICAL SENSATION-EMOTIONAL CORRESPONDENCES:

HOW EMOTIONS AFFECT ENERGY PURIFICATION

Certain emotions – such as anger, pride, triumph, elation and power – naturally cause a rise in your Yang Qi that is most often felt in the upper regions of your body. Yang Qi tends to rise while Yin Qi tends to descend. This is why Vajrayana Buddhism deliberately employs intense emotional states like "divine anger" and "divine pride" in specific meditative and ritual practices. These emotions are not cultivated as personal traits, but are purposefully invoked *to elevate Yang energy* to strongly differentiate it, at those times, from the Yin aspects of your body's Prana. Similarly, higher spiritual beings – Arhats with advanced transcendental bodies – will often provoke similar Yang emotions in practitioners when they seek to cleanse or refine their Yang Qi for the purposes of spiritual ascension.

In both Eastern and Western traditions, another common technique is to grant individuals ecstatic *states of ecstasy or ecstatic visions* of heavenly realms or divine beings – a method frequently seen in Christian mysticism – which temporarily raises and expands the practitioner's Yang energy. This was often done for the Hindu saint, **Sri Ramakrishna Paramahansa**, who was frequently given elevating visions to raise his Yang Prana. In *The Visions of Ramakrishna*, it is explained:

> Most of his visions, especially of the Mother, were of great beauty. Swami Saradananda tells us that Sri Ramakrishna saw at this time limitless forms of the Devi, from the two-armed to the ten-armed. The Master himself speaks of meditating under the tree when 'Sin' appeared before him and tempted him in various ways. It came in the form of an English soldier (pointed symbolism!) wanting to give wealth, honour, sex pleasure, occult powers, etc. 'I began to pray to the Divine Mother! I still remember that form of the Mother, Her world-bewitching beauty. She came to me taking the form of Krishnamayi, but it was as if Her glance moved the world.' The most beautiful of all these visions, he said, was that of Raja-rajesvari, 'Queen of queens,' one of the traditional ten forms of the Divine Mother, who is also known as Sodasi. 'It looked,' he said, trying to put this into language, 'as if the beauty of the person of Sodasi had got melted, spread all around, and was illumining the universe in all directions.' ...

In this period, the close of Tantric sadhana, the Master had visions also of various male figures such Bhairava, companion of Siva; under the vilva-tree where most of these practices were undertaken, he had many 'flaming visions' and other mystical experiences the contents of which he was not able to reveal.

'There were then so many extraordinary visions and experiences in the Master's life day after day,' says Swami Saradananda, 'that it is beyond the power of man to mention all of them.'[9]

A wide range of uplifting emotions and activities – such as anger, pride, courage, triumph, heroism, confidence, victory, domination, euphoria, sexual excitement, joy, optimism, love, amusement, willpower, mirth, brightness, aliveness and vitality – naturally stimulate and elevate the body's Yang Qi. These energies are also aroused through external circumstances like weddings, festivals, sunshine visualizations, active physical exercise, masculinity rites, pranayama (breathwork), and favorable planetary influences. In essence, anything that invigorates your body-mind with vitality helps to raise Yang energy.

The basic Prana purification technique of all spiritual schools is to have you entertain a *dominant attitude* or *strong emotional state* (e.g., hope, love, care, joy, etc.) that thereby arouses *sensations* inside your body that are connected with arousing your Yang Qi or Yin Qi. You are put into situations or perform exercises that evoke strong emotional states to activate Prana.

As an example, during sexual intercourse the happiness, excitement, joy and pleasurable feelings of sex can envelop you completely, and if you understand this then you can use its ability to stir the full energy of your body as a pathway for inner Qi cultivation. This is the basis of tantric sex practice. If you hold onto strong elevated emotions when doing powerful breathing exercises, you can charge your body in that way as well.

During kundalini purification, many traditions use exercises or situations to intentionally provoke strong Yin emotional states – especially fear, sadness, and anxiety – to stimulate and isolate the Yin energy for refinement. There is no mystery behind this method. Enlightened masters

---

[9] *The Visions of Sri Ramakrishna*, Swami Yogeshananda, (Sri Ramakrishna Math, Chennai: India), pp. 43-45.

deliberately place the practitioner in emotionally challenging or frightening situations, because such states intensify Yin Qi, making it more distinct from the body's mixed, undifferentiated energy field, and therefore easier to purify.

The "Yin-raising" emotions commonly include fright, shock, grief, anxiety, sadness, worry, sullenness, disappointment, loneliness, isolation, hopelessness, helplessness, resignation, vulnerability, rejection, obedience or subservience, inner turmoil and travail, physical pain, intimidation, humility, self-surrender, yearning, hunger (fasting), depression, guilt, embarrassment, shame, humiliation, apathy, disgust, revulsion, jealousy, treachery, sneakiness, and greed. The same goes for feeling unwanted, feeling let down, feeling confused and lost, feeling unimportant or inferior or insignificant, or feeling on guard (anxious) and nervously uncomfortable.

If you experience sickness, chills or the flu, or visit environments known to be full of Yin Prana (such as hospitals, cremation grounds, ossuaries, etcetera) this will also stimulate or raise your Yin Prana.

Therefore, during the kundalini purification process, in many traditions the spiritual masters guiding the procedure will try to strongly arouse your Yin energy by using great fright, disgust, sickness, anxiety or depression, and so forth. There is no special magic behind this.

The enlightened masters will commonly put you into situations where you will likely become very afraid since fear and anxiety arouse your Yin energy, and fear or anxiety or guilt is one of the easiest ways to evoke that energy. During those times it becomes easier to purify that negative energy because in being stimulated it becomes more differentiated from the rest of your body's energy, and thus it becomes easier to isolate and purify.

Various spiritual paths illustrate this with striking practices:

- In Japanese Shugendo, adherents are hung upside down from cliffs to activate their Yin Qi through fear and disorientation. They also bathe in cold waterfalls to stimulate Yin Qi.
- The Aghori Shaivite tradition uses cremation grounds, ghost mantras, and meditations on corpses to instill fear and revulsion in practitioners, catalyzing deep Yin purification.
- In the Tibetan Chöd tradition, practitioners confront demons and spirits to deliberately induce fright for the same purpose.

- Christian monastics are often overwhelmed with visions of demons that evoke fear or terror; thoughts of sin or hellish retribution; or experience sorrow and sadness from laboring in ossuaries surrounded by bones because these ;settings and emotions will stimulate Yin Prana into arising.

Across traditions, the most reliable and effective method for purifying Yin energy is to provoke deep fear or emotional distress. This spiritual strategy, though often misunderstood, is a time-honored technique for catalyzing energetic transformations by subjecting individuals to special human experiences that provoke fear.

THE DEMON MASQUERADE – EXPLAINING SPIRITUAL WARFARE EXPERIENCES

One vivid example comes from **Saint Paisios of Mount Athos**, who described undergoing intense spiritual warfare during a period of solitude that coincided with his kundalini purification process. In 1962, while living as a hermit near Saint Catherine's Monastery in the Sinai Desert, Paisios entered a profound phase of inner conflict designed to raise his Yin Qi. During one particular two-week retreat in a small *asketerion* (hermitage) perched above the monastery, he endured such fierce spiritual trials and warfare with the devil that he later told his fellow monks: "What I experienced up there from the devil in those fifteen days cannot be expressed. It is impossible to imagine. I felt as if I was nailed to the Cross." In a Russian Youtube video with English subtitles ("St. Catherine's Monastery: St. Paisios at Sinai") he describes some of those spiritual struggles.

Saint Paisios reported that the devil himself materialized and battled with him in a great spiritual struggle. In truth, this terrifying encounter was not a demonic assault, but rather the materialization of a *nirmanakaya* emanation from an enlightened spiritual master, who made him think it was the devil to provoke an intense Yin Prana purification. The purpose of these onslaughts was that the masters guiding his kundalini transformations saw this as an opportunity for intense Yin Prana purification, and fright was used to raise and thus differentiate his Yin Prana from Yang Prana.

Saint Paisios reported many physical attacks by demons during the earliest stages of this purification process, including being thrown across the room while praying. On one occasion, he described a demonic serpent attempting to strangle him, which he overcame by reciting the Jesus Prayer. Actually, these were "good guys" masquerading as "bad guys" in order to help complete his purification process so that he could ascend to a higher stage of spiritual attainment.

The Taoist immortal **Lu Dongbin** and Tibetan yogini **Yeshe Tsogyal** both described enduring intense battles with devils and demons during their spiritual journeys. In truth, these terrifying encounters were not attacks by evil forces, but rather divine intercessions – enlightened beings in disguise, deliberately provoking fear in order to stimulate and purify their Yin Prana through emotional shock and inner upheaval.

Yeshe Tsogyel wrote about a time she spent in retreat when, "Again a variety of shapes and forms appeared. Many limbs without bodies hung in space before me. Many exceedingly repulsive forms flashed in and out of my vision, writhing around in spectral configurations in space. An enormous head without a body, its upper jaw lost in the clouds and its lower jaw resting on the ground its tongue lolling in between, its fangs gleaming white, approached closer and closer. Other violent forms also appeared: within a castle the size of a mustard seed many men struggled and fought; fires blazed, floods poured forth, landslides hurtled down, tress fell, gales blew, etc., but always I would sit unmoving in vajra-like *samadhi*, and the forms would vanish." (*Sky Dancer: The Secret Life and Songs of the Lady Yeshe Tsogyel*)

Padre Pio, the renowned Capuchin friar and mystic, frequently recounted intense spiritual battles with demonic forces throughout his life. Among these harrowing experiences were encounters with apparitions of black dogs, which he interpreted as manifestations of the devil. In one particularly vivid account from his early years at San Giovanni Rotondo, Padre Pio described being alone in the choir late at night when he was confronted by a demon in the guise of a huge black dog. He attempted to invoke the name of Jesus but found himself unable to speak or breathe, feeling as though he was on the verge of death. Only after mentally calling upon Jesus did the oppressive presence vanish, and the air cleared. These terrifying visions were not isolated incidents. Padre Pio often reported that the devil appeared to him in various forms, including as a black cat or other repugnant animals, with the intent to instill fear and disrupt his spiritual focus. These visions were given to him, of course, in order to put him into a stage of heightened fear and fright so that higher powers might better isolate and purify his Yin Qi (Prana).

Such assaults will happen to all people going through the kundalini purification process, but they always last for only a short period of time. They have one major purpose, which is to help purify the practitioner's Yin Prana through an intense emotional stimulation that arouses one's Yin Qi, and then there is a washing of that Qi to cleanse it.

Xuanzang (602-664), the renowned Chinese Buddhist monk who traveled to India in the 7th century, also reported facing numerous demonic trials during his arduous journey across the harsh Central Asian deserts, during which time he was passing through the kundalini process. One of the most famous accounts describes his experience crossing the Taklamakan Desert, where he became separated from his caravan and found himself alone in the vast, waterless expanse. As he trudged through the shifting sands for days without water, Xuanzang began experiencing what he interpreted as demonic apparitions – ghostly figures, mirages of cities and oases, and terrifying creatures designed to lead him astray or drive him to despair.

During these trials, Xuanzang relied heavily on the recitation of the *Diamond Sutra* (*Vajracchedika Prajnaparamita Sutra*) to protect himself from demonic forces. According to his own travel memoir, the *Record of the Western Regions*, and other historical accounts, he would chant passages from this sutra continuously as protection against the supernatural entities that seemed to multiply in the desert's isolation. When demons appeared as seductive figures promising water and rest, or as fearsome beasts threatening to devour him, Xuanzang would increase his recitation, particularly focusing on passages about emptiness and the illusory nature of phenomena – core teachings of the *Diamond Sutra* that helped him recognize these apparitions as ultimately unreal.

The most dramatic incident occurred when Xuanzang, nearly dying of thirst, encountered a particularly persistent demon who took the form of a beautiful woman offering water from a crystal pitcher. As he raised the vessel to his lips, Xuanzang recognized the demonic nature of the apparition and began reciting the *Diamond Sutra* with renewed vigor. According to the account, the demon shrieked and fled as he chanted the famous passage: "All conditioned phenomena are like dreams, illusions, bubbles, shadows, dew, or lightning; contemplate them thus." This powerful recitation not only dispelled the immediate threat but also helped sustain him until he eventually found real water and rejoined his companions. Throughout the remainder of his journey, Xuanzang continued to use the *Diamond Sutra* as his primary weapon against demonic forces, combining it with other Buddhist practices like visualization and mindfulness meditation to overcome the various supernatural challenges he encountered in mountains, forests, and remote regions along the Silk Road.

While you can find many cases of "demonic assaults" in Hindu, Buddhist, Taoist, Jewish, Moslem, Christian and other literature, the most detailed accounts are usually found in the hagiographies of various Christian saints (e.g., Athanasius' *Life of St. Antony*, Gregory's *Dialogues*) and desert father literature (e.g., *Sayings of the Desert Fathers*). Some of the most famous accounts concern **Saint Anthony the Great** (251-356), who spent twenty years in the Egyptian desert where demons attacked him in the forms of wild beasts, terrifying apparitions, and seductive women.

Saint Anthony was constantly tempted with visions of wealth, doubts about his faith, and lustful thoughts, but he resisted everything through prayer, fasting, and the sign of the cross. If you read his accounts carefully you will note that some of his encounters were designed to stimulate great fear (and thus his body's Yin Prana), some raised the emotion of greed (which stimulated Yin Prana), and some his sexual desire (which would raise his Yang Prana that would then wash the Prana of his penis that normally has low Qi circulation unless aroused), and so forth.

The Tibetan yogini **Yeshe Tsogyel** was also accosted by visions that served to raise her sexual desire, proving that both men and women are attacked in this manner as just another way, out of many, targeted at raising their Yang Qi. Her biography recounts,

On another occasion, the spirits took the form of a band of

handsome youths, their faces beautiful and complexions wholesome, good to smell, well built and sturdy – a joy to look upon. To begin with they spoke to her respectfully, addressing her as "Mistress" and "Lady," but later they called her "girl" and "Tsogyal," and began to speak to her with words of desire. They started by teasing her playfully, but little by little they uncovered their manhood, saying things like, 'Hey, girl, is this what you want? Do you want its milk?' And they put their arms around her waist, fondling her breasts, playing with her sexual parts, kissing her, making love in all sorts of ways. Some of the young men disappeared, subdued by strength of the Lady's concentration. Others, through the concentration that perceives all things as illusion, faded away, mere phantoms. Still others, through the counteractive meditation of a Bodhisattva, were changed into blackened corpses, hideous old men, lepers, blind men, cripples, and idiots, all of them loathsome. And being thus transformed, they disappeared.[10]

While founding his monastery, **Saint Benedict of Nursia** (480–547 AD), the founder of western monasticism, faced similar episodes of demonic opposition, as well as visions of lustful women sent to tempt him and his monks. He overcame these through prayer and mortification, famously rolling in thorns to subdue his flesh. Beyond the initial temptations of lustful visions, historical accounts record several intense confrontations with evil forces. When he first retreated to his cave in Subiaco, demons repeatedly attempted to frighten him with terrifying apparitions and disturbing noises designed to drive him from his place of prayer and contemplation.

Saint Benedict faced numerous episodes of demonic opposition throughout his spiritual journey, but the most famous incident occurred when a particularly powerful demon took the form of a beautiful woman who appeared before Benedict, attempting to seduce him through her physical allure. This vision was so vivid and compelling that Benedict, recognizing the danger to his chastity, threw himself into a nearby thicket of

---

[10] *Lady of the Lotus-Born: The Life and Enlightenment of Yeshe Tsogyal*, Gyalwa Changchub and Namkhai Nyingpo, trans. by The Padmakara Translation Group, (Shambhala, Boston, 1999), p. 84.

thorns and nettles, rolling among them until his body was lacerated and bleeding. Through this self-mortification, he permanently conquered the demon of lust, later stating that the physical pain helped him overcome the spiritual temptation.

St. Pachomius (c. 292–348), the father of communal monasticism, faced extensive demonic opposition as he established Egypt's first organized monastic communities. Throughout his life, demons attacked him with countless apparitions, including visions of pagan gods from his pre-Christian days, grotesque and terrifying creatures, and deceptive images designed to undermine his faith and corrupt his monks. These supernatural assaults often occurred during prayer, at night in his cell, and particularly when he was making crucial decisions about the monastic rules that would govern his communities for generations.

One particularly detailed account from the Life of Pachomius describes how demons repeatedly appeared to him in the guise of seductive figures – both male and female – attempting to lure him into sin through appeals to his senses and memories of worldly pleasures. These tempting apparitions were often accompanied by vivid sensory experiences: perfumed scents, soft voices calling his name, and tactile sensations designed to awaken carnal desires. When these failed, the demons would transform into terrifying beasts or appear as angry pagan deities threatening divine punishment if he abandoned traditional Egyptian religious practices. Pachomius consistently overcame these attacks through prolonged prayer, fasting, and by gathering his monks for communal worship, finding that group spiritual warfare proved more powerful than individual resistance alone.

The Russian mystic, **St. Seraphim of Sarov** (1754–1833), also endured extraordinary demonic persecution throughout his spiritual life, with attacks intensifying during periods of intense prayer and asceticism. During his legendary 1,000-day continuous prayer vigil performed on a rock in the forest near his hermitage, he experienced repeated violent attacks from demons who appeared wielding physical weapons. These evil spirits manifested as dark, menacing figures brandishing axes, clubs, and heavy logs, which they hurled at him with supernatural force, yet miraculously, despite the ferocity of these assaults, Seraphim remained completely unharmed. Witnesses who discovered the scene after such attacks reported finding the forest floor littered with broken weapons and splintered wood, while Seraphim himself bore no marks or injuries from what appeared to have been vicious battles.

Beyond these dramatic physical assaults, Seraphim regularly encountered demons in the form of large black dogs that would prowl around his hermitage, especially during his long nights of prayer. These spectral canines would circle him menacingly, emitting otherworldly howls designed to frighten him, and attempted to place themselves between him and his prayer corner. According to his own accounts, these demon-dogs would sometimes take on grotesque hybrid forms – appearing with human faces or multiple heads – and would speak in human voices, taunting him with blasphemies or trying to convince him that his rigorous asceticism was prideful rather than holy. In his letters and conversations with spiritual children, Seraphim explained that these canine manifestations were particularly cunning because they exploited the natural human affection for dogs, hoping to distract him through seemingly innocent appearances before revealing their true demonic nature.

As to **St. Padre Pio**, whom we always seem to return to since his case is so well documented, in letters written between 1910 and 1916 to Fr. Agostino and Fr. Benedetto, he described frequent demonic assaults, including visions designed to provoke his lust. These visions were not detailed explicitly but implied sexual content, such as provocative female figures meant to arouse his sexual desires. Padre Pio reported that the devil appeared in "impure forms" or presented "indecent images" to tempt him, often during prayer or sleep.

Pio noted that these temptations were most intense early in his priesthood, particularly around the time he received the stigmata (1918). The reason they mostly appeared in his early priesthood, before he started showing miraculous abilities, was because this was when he was going through the internal Prana purification process to achieve the subtle body achievement, or first stage of Arhatship. He described the devil's tactics as relentless, aiming to exploit human weakness, but affirmed that his devotion to Mary and Christ prevented him from succumbing to all the challenges and temptations that would often disappear once confronted.

You must remember that for most monks and nuns of any spiritual tradition, the visions they see when going through the troublesome kundalini purification process are designed to strongly arouse either their Yin Prana (through fright, humility, embarrassment, sadness, depression, sickness, etc.) or Yang Prana (through sexual lust, raising of pride, ambition, courage, anger, etc.). This happens for Jewish rabbis going through the process, Muslim clerics, and the holy men of every spiritual tradition. This is not restricted to the practitioners of one religions, or one small subset of religions alone. Everyone goes through this process.

This is a bothersome process that all spiritual adherents must go through because your own emotional reactions, and the corresponding physical energies, must be stoked to rise up while spiritual beings then wash it with their own energies. Only by provoking strong emotions can your Yin Qi become strongly separated (differentiated) from your Yang Qi sufficiently, and then worked on for purification purposes.

The methods used as spiritual assaults to your emotions will differ by tradition, and it bodes well to *have an enlightened spiritual master nearby* who will protect you from the extremes of the process. Spiritual practitioners will dangerously experience all sorts of degrees of temptations, fearful illusions, threatening sounds, or painful feelings to stimulate their Yin Qi. All the higher masters want to show off their skills to their colleagues in creating metal apparitions during this process. This is a terrible time where you will get pummeled so much that no deva who is watching your progress will ask with jealousy, "Why does he get helped to attain the higher bodies and not me?" Usually they'll just laugh at you because they know it is actually a helpful process, and they are often going through something similar as well.

It is also best if you go through this process while living in the remote countryside rather than live in a major city because being readily available to city devas will certainly mean extra visitors, along with more troubles due to the extra visitor volume. Even though you do go into retreat in the countryside, devas will still travel to you in groups with their masters because they want purifying work done on their bodies so that they can attain the Causal body. In a local region, you become the center of this process.

It is also dangerous to go through the kundalini purification process while living under a *Saturn, Mars, Neptune, Pluto or Uranus astrolocality line!*[11] The best line to live under is a Jupiter line, then Venus or Mercury line. A dry, arid climate is also better than a wet, humid climate, and the perfect situation is you want to be living with or near an enlightened spiritual master, or in/near a monastery with a long tradition of saints or enlightened adepts.

At various stages of the process, a saint-to-be will often suffer from lots of "fairy brushing" where spiritual entities will lightly brush their face using their own Qi to demonstrate their "lightness" *siddhi* skills to their own teachers. The annoying sensation of fairy brushing will feel as if a spider's web covers your face or tickling ants swarm over it from your forehead to the bridge of the nose, eye sockets, cheeks, jaws, teeth and mouth or ears. This will irritate you tremendously, especially when it goes in and out of the ears. You can wear a balaclava face mask when going through the process to counteract the attacks by deadening the sensations, and you can put vibrators on certain body parts when they are attacked with pain or irritation, which especially happens to body parts you cannot easily reach. The kundalini transformation process is a very abusive process, which is why no one wants to speak about it since the information might dissuade people from becoming spiritual practitioners.

In particular you will be attacked on your face, in your nose and ears, at the nerves under the teeth, in and around your asshole, *on the right side of your body* and on the muscles running along the right knee. The momentary removal of the strength of your ankles that is immediately restored, unexplained fits of sneezing, pressure on or in the head, and all sorts of other sensations will be experienced because spiritual masters will want to use you to demonstrate the level of their skills to their colleagues or superiors. They have to demonstrate how capable they are at manipulating the heaviness or lightness of the energy of multiple *nirmanakaya* projections on you, the devas present, the Casual-bodied attendees, and others attending your session. The more *nirmanakaya* you can simultaneously handle skillfully, the higher your ranking in the heavenly hierarchy, and you are one of the situations where spiritual masters test their skills against one another.

Everyone going through the process will experience completely

---

[11] See the *Geostel Brownbook*, by Julian Lee, for basic information on astrolocality lines.

different visions and physical sensations than others suffering through it under different masters in different regions, which is why the process seems unrecognizable across traditions. It is not standardized because each group responsible for helping an individual achieve the glorification (deification or divinization) of attaining the deva body, and the local devas as well, has their own traditional way of managing the kundalini purification process.

Every spiritual school tests their senior masters on their ability to use numerous *nirmanakaya* emanations during this time, and you will suffer when they do this because they will give various types of pain to you and to the entire audience attending one of your purification sessions. Pain drives away devas who haven't worked hard enough at mastering the eight *siddhis* and are not yet ready to ascend, and is also the easiest way to provoke a group response so that everyone can see how well you can control your *nirmanakaya* projections.

This short synopsis might enable you to realize that countless spiritual practices, most of which fall under the umbrella of "spiritual cultivation," are designed to help you purify the Prana of your inner subtle body, but in disguise. The task that needs to be done basically entails differentiating the purest or highest-grade energy of your body from the densest, most impure, or lowest grade energy, and in particular, differentiating Yin from Yang Prana as well.

This is one reason that Orthodox Christian monks are taught obedience and humility, which tends to purify your Yin Qi. When many start crying endless tears over their sins, world suffering and other issues this sadness is also a time when their Yin Qi becomes predominant and can be purified more easily, so you will find this practice with many Orthodox Fathers. Such practices essentially involve differentiating the Yin and Yang Pranas of your body from one another and refining (purifying) the nature of your Prana in general.

A SUMMARY OF COMMONALITIES

As we conclude our examination of incorruptibility across spiritual traditions, several profound truths emerge. First, this phenomenon transcends religious boundaries, appearing with remarkable consistency across Christian, Buddhist, Hindu, Taoist, and other spiritual paths.

The phenomenon is also recognized in Islam, as the hadith Sahih Hadith 1887 (from *Sahih Muslin*) states that martyrs' bodies do not decompose ("The earth does not consume the bodies of the prophets") and **Ibn Hibban** (c. 884-965) claims that prophets' bodies do not decompose. The tomb of **Imam Ali** (c. 599-661) in Najaf was allegedly found intact when relocated, and some legends claim that Abdul-Qadir Gilani's body when exhumed was found uncorrupted.

The phenomenon is no doubt present in Judaism as well, but Jewish burial law requires natural decomposition, so we cannot confirm cases such as that of modern rabbis or even **Rabbi Yehuda HaNasi** (Judah the Prince, 2nd century) where legends say his body was temporarily preserved.

The similarities in all these reported cases – bodies remaining flexible, emitting fragrance, and resisting decomposition – suggest a universal physiological transformation rather than coincidental preservation. Like bilocation, the phenomenon appears across the world's religions to the most devoted of spiritual practitioners who were also known for their virtue and pure conduct.

Incorruptibility consistently correlates with intense spiritual practice. Whether through Christian contemplative prayer, Buddhist meditation, Hindu yoga, or Taoist internal alchemy, the individuals who achieve this state invariably devoted decades to rigorous spiritual disciplines. Many became known as saints or gurus or sages. This correlation strongly suggests that the transformation of the physical body is directly linked to dedicated spiritual practices.

Third, the process of kundalini purification, while described in different terminologies across traditions, follows remarkably similar patterns worldwide. The reports of intense heat, cold, energy movements, and emotional challenges appear consistently whether described by Desert Fathers, Tibetan yogis, Buddhist monks, Hindu gurus, Jewish rabbis, Sufi saints, or Taoist adepts. These universal elements suggest we are observing a single phenomenon interpreted through different cultural and religious lenses.

Perhaps most significantly, the understanding that incorruptibility results from attaining higher spiritual bodies provides *a coherent explanation* for the phenomenon of bilocation discussed in our previous chapter, not to mention the fact that some traditions even tell you the stage of attainment at which it becomes possible.

Furthermore, the same saints whose bodies resist decay after death are often those who demonstrated the ability to appear in multiple places during life. Both abilities appear to stem from the same source – the purification and transformation of the body's inner vital energy (Prana/Qi) through years of dedicated spiritual practice, along with divine assistance.

As to the actual stages of transformation achievements that happen to you over the years as your inner Prana becomes cleansed, the Greeks encoded this information in the legend of the Twelve Labors of Hercules, and you can find several important, recognizable milestones of the purification process explained in *The Little Book of Hercules*. However, the emotional-Prana purification interconnection is most fully revealed in the *Surangama Sutra* of Buddhism.

For those on the spiritual path, these cases of incorruptibility offer both inspiration and caution. They reveal the extraordinary possibilities of human spiritual development while honestly acknowledging the challenges of the purification process since individuals going through the procedure will go through periods of great pain, fear and other forms of suffering.

The message seems clear, however: the transformation of spiritual consciousness and human behavior ultimately extends to the transformation of the physical vessel itself and its inner vital energy or life force (Prana/Qi), pointing toward the ancient wisdom that true spirituality encompasses the whole person – body, energy, and spirit – in its quest for transcendence.

As both science and spirituality continue to evolve, perhaps these remarkable cases will someday bridge the apparent gap between material and spiritual understanding, suggesting that the human being contains ascendency possibilities far beyond our current comprehension – potentials that the saints and sages of every tradition have been demonstrating throughout human history.

CHAPTER 5:
12+ YEARS OF INTERNAL ENERGY CLEANSING

The Hindu epic tale of *Samudra Manthana* within the *Vishnu Purana* – the "Churning of the Ocean of Milk" – serves as a profound allegory for the process of kundalini washing which individuals must go through in order to become saints. This story isn't mythology – it's a detailed blueprint for the internal process people pass through that transforms your internal subtle energy into something transcendent. Just as the gods and demons churned the ocean of milk in this story to extract the nectar of immortality (*amrita*), so too must seekers undergo an intense inner stirring process to purify their inner vital energies (Prana, Qi, kundalini, life force, subtle body) to attain the transcendental spiritual bodies of liberation.

There is a lot of work that goes into the alchemy of spiritual purification, and a lot of inner turmoil that saints must pass through in order to benefit from the inner alchemy of kundalini washing. The *Vishnu Purana* symbolizes the multi-year kundalini purification process that saints go through to purify their vital energies and attain the transcendental energy bodies above the realm of matter.

In other words, it teaches how kundalini alchemy purifies the body's energy for liberation, and communicates the actual mechanics of spiritual emergence: the stirring of latent vital forces within the body, the dissolution of impurities, and the ultimate distillation of a purified spirit body due to the frictional churning process.

STIRRING THE "OCEAN OF MILK"

In this story, the Milky Ocean represents your physical body, composed of 70% water and born from milky semen, together with the life force energies of your higher spiritual bodies condensed within it. When this ocean is churned, it produces *amrita* – the elixir of immortality that symbolizes your refined spiritual energy – particularly the subtle energy "deva body" that can survive for centuries, so the story is really about internally spinning, revolving or rotating the Qi/Prana of your body for years to produce the liberation of your subtle body. Taoism calls this rotation of inner Qi a "macrocosmic" or "microcosmic" circulation.

The churning of the Ocean of Milk mirrors how spiritual practices separate your life force energy (Prana/Qi) into pure and impure components. Just as continuous stirring separates butter from milk, sustained spiritual work of revolving your Prana gradually purifies your inner energy until it can separate from your physical form. Through spiritual practices that "stir" our inner energy (Prana), which we experience as rotations of energy inside us, we gradually purify and differentiate our inner subtle body for its eventual escape from the physical shell. This is why saints will feel waves of energy rolling around inside themselves for years, revolving through different orbits or regions of their body, during a kundalini purification process. It is basically a process of energy refinement through frictional purification, which involves cleansing our own Prana by scrubbing it with the Prana of another.

The *Samudra Manthana* churning of the Ocean of Milk therefore represents the multi-year process of kundalini purification that is performed upon saints who have devoted themselves to (1) becoming highly virtuous in their behavior and thinking, and (2) deeply practicing religious exercises. As your body's internal energies are "churned," which Christians usually identify as "the Holy Spirit is felt inside me," your emotions will rise and fall and this turmoil will change the quality of your inner energy in tune with the emotions.

After years of this internal washing – while suffering various extremes of intense emotions – your inner subtle energetic body can eventually purify and then separate itself off from the other impure physical energies of the human body. In the *Samudra Manthana* story, the devas represent your pure energies, or Yang Prana, while asuras represent your impure energies, or Yin Prana. Both have to be stirred during the process, whereas in the story both do the stirring.

Spiritual traditions describe this inner alchemy of spiritual purification in various ways: separating from or ascending above your animal nature; purifying the body's vital energy so that its most refined aspect can disconnect from, untangle from, or separate out from the rest of the body's vital force; differentiating lower from higher (impure and pure) body energies; raising the vibrational frequency of one's purest life force energy so that it can become liberated from its shell; refining your energy to produce a perfected astral copy of your physical form, etcetera.

Through continuous energy rotation over years, your life force gradually becomes more distinguished and refined compared to the untransformed, impure energies that bind it to your body. Imagine stirring a tub of muddy water – the center becomes clearer and more fluid while thicker muddier sediment clings to the edges. Since the residues sticking to the sides become more viscous and solid, we can definitely say that a differentiation of quality or purity occurs.

Similarly, as your central life force (Prana) becomes more refined and distinguished from the unpurified transitional Prana within you (that attaches Prana to your atoms or cells), the bond between your body and your purified Prana weakens. Separation then becomes possible – something that normally occurs only at death. A thin connection usually remains when the astral body separates, like stretched taffy between the physical and subtle bodies, yet the subtle body possesses far greater etheric refinement than the more viscous (impure) Prana that remains animating the physical form. All your spiritual bodies are connected to one another this way with the entire network called a *sambhogakaya* in Buddhism.

In the *Samudra Manthana*, Mount Mandara serves as the stirring rod, while gods (devas) and demons (asuras) must churn the ocean for an extremely long time, indicating that this purification work on the human body requires years before a higher deva body can ascend out of it. Hinduism teaches that a minimum of twelve years is required, usually extending much longer. This explains why saints remain deep in prayer and spiritual practice for well over a decade, always under the guidance and protection of accomplished masters who know what is going on and supervise the entire process. After achieving the subtle body, practitioners will often relocate to work with different masters in other regions to finish what is required for the next body achievement. That helps the local devas in a new area as well. Each new spiritual body requires approximately three years of intensive churning or rotational effort.

Both devas and asuras participated in the churning, representing that both positive and negative energies (both Yin and Yang Prana) must be purified. However, only the devas receive the final *amrita*, symbolizing that only those with virtuous qualities will achieve the higher spiritual bodies. Those dominated by lower impulses – greed, hate, selfishness, violence, ego and carnal desires etc. – cannot achieve the higher transcendental bodies until they purify these harmful traits through ardent spiritual practices.

During the churning process, poison (*halahala*) emerges, representing the toxins and impurities released during purification stages. This explains why people undergoing kundalini transformations often experience physical symptoms like skin problems and various illnesses, which are signs of detoxification since poisons are expelled from the body. The Tibetan yogini Yeshe Tsogyel temporarily developed a stammer, had blood and pus ooze from a rent in her neck, and suffered various painful swellings of blood and pus. Many Christian neophyte monks become ill and are sent home to rest and recover during the early stages of the process.

As to the Ocean of Milk, the churning eventually produced wonderful treasures:

- *Ucchaishrava*, a seven-headed flying horse (representing the entire purified subtle body of the saint with its seven chakras)
- *Kamadhenu* or *Surabhi*, the wish-fulfilling cow (symbolizing the purified brain of the saint)
- *Kalpavriksha*, the wish-fulfilling tree (representing the purified nervous system of the saint)
- *Chintamani*, a magical gem (symbolizing the purified brain stem)
- Goddess Lakshmi (of wealth and prosperity), who represents the immense value of the accomplishment of attaining the subtle body

These treasures arising out of the stirred Milek Ocean symbolize the purified subtle body that arises out of this process of internal alchemy of Qi rotations. This transformation doesn't happen in isolation – it requires support from higher spiritual beings who must lend their energies to actually perform the purifying process, which lasts for years. The list of individuals who achieved incorrupt bodies or who could perform bilocation readily revealed that they were all highly moral, virtuous individuals, meaning that they merited it, as well as ardent practitioners of spiritual efforts, which helps with the process.

Developing a higher spiritual body means liberating refined spiritual energy from its denser physical nature. This requires "churning" or revolving the energies within your physical body through your own efforts together with the cooperation of countless enlightened masters (the "union of saints"). These beings typically work on helping multiple deva aspirants in your local area simultaneously because the process demands tremendous collective energy and commitment, so it is best to help an entire group of individuals arise rather than just one. The process is lengthy and demanding. If your spiritual merit is insufficient, these helpers won't work on your development as intensely – you must continue purifying your mind (mental perspectives, thoughts, decisions), behavior and body and accumulating merit until you qualify. When you are ready, and when enough deva students in your region have also attained sufficient merit for earning their Causal bodies, the procedure typically begins for a saint.

The kundalini transformation involves Yang Qi and generates heat through friction, which is why it is often symbolized by fire. This is the yogic "fire of separation" that produces purification and eventually allows the subtle body to detach from its physical form. While you'll usually experience warm energy during the process, you will also experience cold sensations when your Yin energies are being purified, whereas when Yang energies are being used or worked on you will feel warmth.

During kundalini purification, you will experience many different energy sensations within your body. **Swami Muktananda** (1908-1982) reported feeling various sensations of heat or pain at the base of his spine, heaviness in his head, involuntary movements, energy flows throughout his body, unusual breathing patterns, and experienced inner lights, strange sounds, visions, voices and other extraordinary occurrences. Ramana Maharshi wisely cautioned that practitioners might "see bright effulgences, hear unusual sounds, or see visions of gods appearing within or outside themselves. They should not be deceived by these experiences and forget themselves."[12]

---

[12] *The Spiritual Teaching of Ramana Maharshi*, Ramana Maharshi, (Shambhala Publications, Boston, 1988), p. 26.

INCORRUPTIBLE BODIES AND BILOCATION MIRACLES

Ajit Mookerjee once wrote about all sorts of various experiences:

> The ascent of Kundalini as it pierces through the chakras is manifested in certain physical and psychic signs. Yogis have described the trembling of the body which precedes the arousal of Kundalini, and the sensation of heat which passes like a current through the Sushumna channel. During Kundalini's ascent, inner sounds resemble a waterfall, the humming of bees, the sound of a bell, a flute, or the tinkling of ornaments. In closed-eye perception the yogi visualizes a variety of forms, such as dots of light, or geometrical shapes that in the final state of illumination dissolve into an inner radiance of intensely bright, pure light. The aspirant may experience creeping sensations along the spinal cord, tingling sensations all over the body, heaviness in the head or sometimes giddiness, autonomic and involuntary laughing or crying; or he may see visions of deities or saints. Dream scenes of all kinds may appear, from the heavenly to the demonic. Physically, the abdomen wall may become flat and be drawn towards the spine; there may be diarrhea or constipation; the anus contracts and is drawn up; the chin may press down against the neck; the eyeballs roll upwards or rotate; the body may bend forward or back, or even roll around on the floor; breathing may be constricted, (sometimes it seems to cease altogether, although in fact it does not, but merely becomes extremely slight); the mind becomes empty and there is an experience of being a witness in the body.
>
> There may be a feeling of Prana flowing in the brain or spinal cord. Sometimes there is a spontaneous chanting of mantras or songs, or simply vocal noises. The eyes may not open in spite of one's efforts to open them. The body may revolve or twist in all directions. Sometimes it bounces up and down with crossed legs, or creeps about, snake-like, on the floor. Some perform *asanas* (yogic postures) both known and unknown; sometimes the hands move in classic, formal dance patterns, even though the meditator knows nothing of dance. Some speak in tongues.
>
> Sometimes the body feels as if it is floating upwards, and sometimes as if it is being pressed down into the earth. It may feel as if it has grown enormously large, or extremely small. It may

shake and tremble and become limp, or turn as rigid as stone. Some get more appetite, some feel aversion to food. Even when engaged in activities other than meditation, the aspirant who concentrates his mind, experiences the movements of Prana-shakti all over the body, or slight tremors. There may be aches in the body, or a rise or drop in temperature. Some people become lethargic and averse to work. Sometimes the meditator hears buzzing sounds as of blowing conches, or bird-song or ringing-bells. Questions may arise in the mind and be spontaneously answered during meditation.

Sometimes the tongue sticks to the palate or is drawn back towards the throat, or protrudes from the mouth. The throat may get dry or parched. The jaws may become clenched, but after a time they reopen. One may start yawning when one sits for meditation. There may be a feeling of the head becoming separated from the body, or "headlessness." Sometimes one may be able to see things around one even with the eyes closed. Various types of intuitive knowledge may begin. One may see one's own image. One may even see one's own body lying dead. From some or all of these signs, one may know that Kundalini Shakti has become active. The Kundalini produces whatever experiences are necessary for the aspirant's spiritual progress, according to habit-pattern formed by past action.[13]

Sometimes you will hear devas speaking to you, or hear spiritual masters masquerading as deities during this lengthy process. Sometimes they will pretend that they are devils and demons to frighten you. You may see visions that will seem just as real as whatever you see with your physical eyes. Some may even show you events occurring in the outer world. At times, you might be able to see the whole system of nerves, veins, and arteries, the digestive and eliminative tracts in your body in multicolored light, or you might see different forms within your body or within someone else's body.

These experiences are illusions. They are visions projected into your consciousness by enlightened humans using their Supra-Causal or

---

[13] *Ancient Wisdom and Modern Science*, ed. by Stanislov Grof, (SUNY Press, Albany: New York, 1984), pp. 125-127.

Superconsciousness body (or their *nirmanakaya*) to override your perception – essentially impressing images from their minds onto yours. As stated, they accomplish this using their own Arhat body or one of its *nirmanakaya* emanations. The Zen school calls these experiences "mara," or delusions.

Only full Arhats and Great Golden Arhats can project a *nirmanakaya* emanation that can override your consciousness to create these visions. The energy of their higher bodies is more refined than the Qi/Prana powering your consciousness, and are in fact composed of the more foundational energies of consciousness. Thus, they can override your mind to control your consciousness because they are more foundational energies of consciousness. This is how saints and sages give people thoughts or directives.

THE SURANGAMA SUTRA

The most valuable guide for navigating all these experiences comes from Buddhism, which collected together in its teachings many materials from earlier Vedic traditions in India. Specifically, the "Fifty Mara Deva States" chapter of the *Surangama Sutra* provides people with essential guidance for more safely passing through the process that produces the higher transcendental bodies, and we already saw many Buddhists who had achieved incorruptible bodies or who demonstrated the miracle of bilocation, which prove they went through the process. The relevant section of the *Surangama Sutra*, formally titled "The Fifty Mara States of the Five Skandhas Affecting Practitioners During Meditation," offers insights into what happens during this purification process.

The first ten of these fifty Mara (illusion) states describe common experiences that ordinary people typically encounter on the spiritual path regardless of their religion:

- Experiencing unusual internal energy sensations not initiated by yourself
- Having visions of things inside your body
- Seeing the form of a spiritual master's body appear to change shape
- Hearing voices in the sky, or within your head
- Seeing light surrounding objects or living beings

- Seeing amazing objects appear in space
- Experiencing visions of spiritual lands and deities
- Feeling that your body is empty
- Being able to see in the dark
- Witnessing distant events

These categories of experiences are what the *Surangama Sutra* also calls "Mara" – delusionary experiences that are neither real events nor genuine spiritual attainments. They are illusions projected into a practitioner's mind by spiritual masters who have various motivations, including demonstrating their skills to others. When you experience them, you'll likely believe they are real (because you cannot deny having this vivid experience) and may feel you have reached a profound stage of spiritual development, particularly when those who created them are encourage your pride.

Most of the visions and sounds you experience on the spiritual path are "Mara" – illusions or deceptions rather than true events or true spiritual attainments, which is why you cannot experience them consistently or summon them at will. *Meditation Case Studies: Concise Explanations of Phenomena Encountered on the Spiritual Path* explains most of these phenomena and their causes, offering translations of the relevant chapters from the *Surangama Sutra* that detail the stages you go through in attaining the higher spiritual bodies that are called "breaking through the *skandhas*." *The Little Book of Hercules* does not focus on these Mara experiences, but instead explains the actual spiritual stages of progress that you achieve on the spiritual path.

The second set of Mara states in the *Surangama Sutra* provides the essential information we want concerning the kundalini purification process. This text, emerging from ancient India's ascetic traditions, clearly describes what practitioners experience when working to "break free of the form *skandha*" (physical body) to achieve liberation as an independent subtle body – the state that makes one a *Srotapanna* Arhat.

During this twelve-year internal alchemy process, kundalini energy rotates continuously through all your energy meridians throughout your entire body. During this period, enlightened masters guide you through countless emotional experiences – both Yin and Yang – to stimulate different types of energy within you while washing it. They orchestrate countless Yin or Yang emotional experiences to stimulate your inner energy in different ways because *that makes it easier to purify all aspects of your Prana*, which responds differently according to your emotional condition. Your subtle body is made of Prana, so you are washing the fabric of your next spiritual form.

These masters also allow their advanced students to practice giving you various thoughts and sensations during this time, which benefits their own training while contributing to your development through Qi rotations. By helping their own students when working on you, the masters ensure their sacrifice of time helping you serves multiple purposes that help them, too.

10 REPRESENTATIVE SITUATIONS THAT RAISE YOUR YIN OR YANG ENERGY

As stated, the second set of ten Mara states described in the *Surangama Sutra* is the important section pertaining to the actual lengthy kundalini purification process. The Sutra tells us that you'll be provoked into expressing strong emotional states during the process leading to "breaking free of the form *skandha* (physical body)," which means finally achieving the liberated subtle body. It states that some of the various emotional experience you will be put through include:

- Great sadness or pity (Yin)
- Excitement and boldness (Yang)
- Hopelessness and forlornness (Yin)
- Pride and arrogance (Yang)
- Dread, anxiety and distress (Yin)
- Purity, peace and joy (Yang)
- Intense self-satisfaction and feelings of superiority (Yang)
- Infinite lightness and purity (Yang)
- Fear of death or absolute extinction (Yin)
- Boundless love, desire or even lust (Yang)

This list is far from complete, and merely indicates some of the many emotional experiences that will arise during spiritual cultivation. Shakyamuni Buddha emphasized that these emotions will be deliberately provoked within you. The purpose is to stimulate different energies inside you so that they more clearly stand apart from the undifferentiated mass of life force within your body, makings it easier to purify the highlighted Prana. When you focus on a dominant attitude or emotion, your Prana changes, and that specific type of energy – which is the body of your spirit self – requires purification.

If you are fortunate, an enlightened teacher will place you in very Yin environments or have you perform Yin activities that appropriately raise your Yin Prana. For instance, some Christian monasteries have novices work in its hospitals containing sick people, or ossuaries surrounded by bones, since these environments give off strong Yin Qi. Otherwise, the novice must wait for times of illness, which is a time when the body expresses strong Yin Qi, and other situations powerful enough for Yin Prana purification such as intense sadness, depression, guilt or shame, fear and so on.

To understand why heavenly beings and spiritual masters provoke emotions in practitioners, examine again the Finnish thermal heat mapping studies (such as "Bodily Maps of Emotions" by Nummenmaa, Glerean, Hari, and Hietanen, available online). These images show where the sensations of various emotions are felt within the human body. The studies reveal that each emotion excites your inner energy (Prana) differently, changing its tone or quality, with physical reactions felt in specific body regions. This excitation appears strongly in unique areas for different emotions or dominant attitudes. If you arouse a dominant attitude, you will strongly arouse positive (Yang) or negative (Yin) energy/Prana in your body, differentiating it from its complement, and allowing it to be more easily purified in that excited state.

The basic cultivation method of virtually every spiritual school is to enter into emotional states that arouse sensations inside your body and activate your Yin or Yang energy, because that arousal purifies your subtle body energy. When powerful Prana flows are activated – such as when you become extremely frightened or joyous – they wash through your entire body's energy system, which is precisely the goal.

You can enter deep Yang or Yin Prana states through devotional emotions, or by becoming absorbed in self-generated mental attitudes that will stimulate your Prana so powerfully that the emotional-energetic result pervades your entire subtle body. Practices that instruct you to give rise to infinite joy, infinite loving-kindness, boundless compassion, and perfect equanimity use this technique. By embracing or projecting positive "infinite" or "boundless" emotions, you transcend your comfort zone and ego-concepts through a limitless energization. You thereby thoroughly wash your Yang Prana – which is the whole point of the exercise. One of the common experiences of Yang Prana activation is that your salvia becomes sweet ("like wine") for a short period of time intermittently, which is a recognized sign in many traditions.

Basically, you try to strongly exhilarate all the Prana inside your body using boundless emotions. This creates whole-body energization that washes your energy in a flooding manner, which is why you do this. A whole-body energization occurs during intense experiences like sex, the celebration of athletic triumph, musical concert excitement, and many other situations.

From thermal images, you can see that negative emotions – such as fear, guilt, disgust, anxiety, sadness, and depression – stimulate your body's Yin energy. When your Yin energy is being purified, you might feel coolness surrounding you, like the vapor coming off of dry ice, which then rises into the sky. It's like a feeling of light air conditioning surrounding your body – called *ching-an* (lightness and peace) in Taoism – but is actually a blessing from higher spiritual beings helping to wash your Yin Prana. Yin energy is cool, so it is often compared to moonlight and called lunar or feminine energy.

Another sign of Yin Prana purification is a temporary chilling state where your teeth chatter and body shivers, requiring blankets for 15-30 minutes. Unlike illness, this extreme state passes quickly. Feelings of coldness within the body (such as when you become sick) typically indicate Yin Prana arising, and sometimes during spiritual practices you will suddenly feel various types of cold energy washing you that are another type of Yin blessing for your purification efforts. *The Little Book of Hercules* and *Meditation Case Studies* explain some of these conditions.

An expanded list of some emotions that raise your Yin energies includes fear, fright, terror, shock, hurt, anxiety, sadness, worry, sullenness, disappointment, loneliness, isolation, hopelessness, helplessness, resignation, vulnerability, rejection, unimportance or inferiority, insignificance, feeling unwanted, feeling let down, feeling confused and lost, feeling on guard and nervously uncomfortable, inner turmoil and travail, intimidation, humility, self-surrender, yearning, hunger, depression, suicide, guilt, embarrassment, shame, humiliation, grief, apathy, disgust, revulsion, jealousy, treachery, sneakiness, greed, as well as physical conditions like chills or flu.

These attitudes, emotions or conditions are all times when your Yin energies become stronger and thus more differentiated from the Yang energies of your body, which *must happen* for your subtle body – the physical body of your next higher stage of beingness – to become totally purified for emergence. If you are going to achieve the subtle body attainment, you have to go through a wide variety of Yin-producing emotions.

This is why the Tibetan master **Padampa Sangye** (d. 1117) once advised, "Approach whatever you find repulsive. Anything you are attracted to let go of it. Visit cemeteries and places that scare you." If you visit and temporarily stay in such scary or repulsive places, you will arouse your Yin Qi *as is necessary for the achievement of the higher spiritual bodies*. This is also one reason why the Hindu god Shiva, who leads people to enlightenment, is said to dwell in charnel grounds surrounded by ghosts and ghouls. He is always associated with characters having strong Yin Qi to show that you cannot just purify your Yang energy but must deal with your Yin energies too. Some Taoists simply try to absorb Yin energies at special times of the day or during the full moon in order to supplement themselves or wash those energies. The lesson being taught is that you cannot just surround yourself with positive Yang experiences but must experience the unhappy Yin emotions of life in order to purify those internal energies as well.

Spiritual masters often arouse Yin energy in students using fright or disgust by creating situations of intense fear or anxiety so that Yin Prana can be differentiated from the Yang energy in your body. This is why the *Surangama Sutra* mentioned that you would be put through various experiences that would cause Yin (or Yang) energies to arise.

In Orthodox Christianity, monks sometimes accomplish a portion of their Yin Prana purification through crying. When practiced for lengthy periods, this is another method to temporarily raise your Yin Qi for purification purposes, as is adopting attitudes of humility and obedience. Some Orthodox Christian monks weep tears of repentance (feeling sorrow for their sins), tears of intercession (weeping for others' salvation), and tears of compunction (weeping at the awe of God's love). For instance, **St. Siloua the Anthonite** (1866-1938) wept uncontrollably for years after a vision of Christ, **St. Paisios of Mount Athos** (1924-1994) would weep for the spiritual state of humanity and decline of faith in the world, and **St. Arsenios the Great** (4th-5th centuries) spent decades weeping over his sins and the sins of the world, and **St. Ephraim the Syrian** (4th century) would weep tears of repentance.

Similarly, Sri Ramakrishna Paramahansa would cry daily before a statue of Mother Kali with a sense of longing and separation (which would elevate his Yin Prana) saying, "I only want you, don't give me anything else." He also dressed as a woman for a short period to imaginarily assume the feminine energies of Yin inside him as part of his purification work. This principle is also revealed in the Hindu story of Indra with 1,000 eyes, and a scene in the Buddhist *Vimalakirti Sutra* where Shariputra is caused to feel the Yin energies of a woman briefly as his Yin Prana was being purified by an enlightened goddess.

Even the Greek hero Hercules dressed as a woman and performed woman's chores for a year – a story created to teach that even strong male figures must experience and purify their Yin Prana on the spiritual path. The Indian warrior Arjuna, companion of Krishna in the *Mahabaharata*, performed a similar feat by disguising himself as a eunuch dance teacher named Brihannala and living as a woman for one year in the kingdom of Virata, where he served in King Virata's court teaching dance and music to Princess Uttara.

When purifying Yin Prana, masters also sometimes use their own *nirmanakaya* energies to cause physical pain or discomfort inside worthy practitioners. This becomes especially intense during the final years of internal alchemy, when the legs and feet often become extremely cold as Yin Prana is continuously washed in that region (as happened to Zen master Hakuin). This process distresses practitioners who don't understand what's happening, sometimes driving them to consider suicide due to its intensity. This is why most Hindus undergo this process under a living master's supervision.

The Orthodox Christian monks of Mount Athos are taught that negative experiences during the twelve-year kundalini transformation come from devils – adding fear-based Yin Prana to pain-based situations – when actually it's simply a purification process. The fact that they often hear "hordes" of demons, which are the deva students laughing at what's happening to them, helps solidify this belief. When only a neophyte at his training monastery, St. Porphyrios of Kafsokalyvia was told not to read a certain book, but curiosity got the best part of him (since the urge to read it was orchestrated by enlightened monks), and felt deep guilt and remorse for a long period afterwards during which time his teachers – **Elder Panteleimon** (late 19th century) and **Elder Iakovos (Jacob) Tsalikis of Evia** (1920-1991) washed his Yin Prana. For six months, another neophyte monk on Mount Athos had to hide from Greek government officials who had orders to draft him for the army, until the monastery officials finally registered him as a monk thus freeing him from such duty, and during this daily anxiety-ridden period of hiding and worry (that the head monks had orchestrated) his Yin Prana was being washed.

These teachings only explain a portion of what happens during the 12+ years of intense Prana purification, known as a kundalini awakening in the East, where you are put through intense emotional ups and downs in order to wash your Prana to achieve the liberation of an independent subtle body that can roam free of your physical nature.

THE 12 MINOR HARDSHIPS OF NAROPA

This is what happens to a saint in his formative years, though no one understands the process. They perform their religious practices while simultaneously being put through a number of intense emotional experiences that raise their Yin and Yang Prana to help these two energies become differentiated from one another and more easily purified for generating the subtle body. By washing the energies of your subtle body, you are strengthening the integrity of that body. Prana becomes stimulated and washed when strong emotions are aroused inside you that move your Qi energies. The *Surangama Sutra* reveals this to guide practitioners so they don't go astray, and the emotional spiking process is also illustrated in stories from Vajrayana Buddhism and Chinese Taoism.

The story of **Mahasiddha Naropa** (c. 956-1040) from Vajrayana Buddhism provides an excellent illustration of these spiritual principles. Born into a Kashmiri Brahman family, Naropa spent twelve years with his teacher **Tilopa** (988-1069) on the banks of the Bagmati river at Nepal's Pashupatinath Temple before attaining *siddhi* – the subtle body achievement that marks the first stage toward complete liberation (*moksha*). Whenever spiritual texts say a yogi attained *siddhi* it means he attained the subtle deva body achievement. Whenever spiritual texts mention a twelve-year period, they are typically referring to the kundalini purification process even though it usually requires more than twelve years for completion. During that time your Prana undergoes continuous rotations and other manipulations, alternating between heat and coolness together with intense emotional experiences, until you develop an independent subtle body.

The story of the "Twelve Minor Trials (Hardships) of Naropa" recounts various experiences that intensely raised both his Yin and Yang energies before Naropa could meet his master Tilopa. Though few understand the deeper meaning of this story, each shocking encounter served to arouse and purify different aspects of Naropa's internal energies that were then washed with the assistance of spiritual masters. The specific emotions evoked during each trial might be interpreted differently, but the essential teaching remains: emotional priming is necessary to wash and purify your Prana. Let's examine each trial and the energies activated:

First Trial: Naropa encountered a horrifically deformed woman, a limbless leper covered with wounds, who blocked his path and could not move aside. Her condition evoked both disgust and repulsion (stimulating his Yin energy) alongside compassion.

Second Trial: At a river, he came upon a dog infested with lice and maggots devouring its rotting flesh and whimpering in agony. This grisly sight stirred both compassion and revulsion, activating both his Yin and Yang energies.

Third Trial: Naropa met a man who was attempting to play devious tricks on his parents, and who asked Naropa to help him in the scheme. Refusing with righteous criticism and visible disdain at this pitiable situation, Naropa felt his Yin and Yang energies surge powerfully.

Fourth Trial: He came upon an elderly man painstakingly picking lice from his skin, only to crush them between his nails, thus arousing his disgust and compassion.

Fifth Trial: He came upon a man cheerfully tearing apart a corpse for its intestines. This ghastly sight naturally filled Naropa with fear and horror, arousing his Yin Prana.

Sixth Trial: Naropa found a man washing his open stomach wound with water, who requested assistance. Though afraid and repulsed, Naropa also felt compassion, creating a powerful confluence of Yin and Yang energies within him.

Seventh Trial: Naropa came upon a great city and asked the king for Tilopa's whereabouts. The king said he would tell Naropa if he married his daughter, but before he could agree, the king withdrew his daughter and locked Naropa inside the room, symbolizing the prison of sexual desire (Yang energy). Naropa then escaped.

Eighth Trial: A hunter with hounds invited Naropa to join the hunt, triggering moral abhorrence for the cruelty of killing (Yin Prana). Naropa declined and continued his journey.

Ninth Trial: By a lake, a couple offered Naropa some non-vegetarian food which he refused. Enraged, the man threatened to kill Naropa's parents. This unpredictable hostility frightened Naropa, immediately arousing his Yin Prana in a strong way.

Tenth Trial: Naropa witnessed a horrifying scene: a man had impaled his father on a stake and imprisoned his mother in a dungeon. Both parents begged Naropa for rescue from their murderous son. Their misery filled him with fear, anxiety, and indignation, thoroughly evoking his Yin Prana due to these strong emotions.

Eleventh Trial: Arriving at a hermitage, Naropa received an elaborate welcome because of his status, thus inflating his pride (and raising his Yang energy). There he saw a beggar named Tilopa (the same name as the master he was seeking) cooking fish while being beaten by the residents. Tilopa's mysterious behavior and teachings left Naropa confused and perplexed, thus arousing his inner Yin energy once again.

Twelfth Trial: Naropa entered a vast plain inhabited by people with strange physical abnormalities. These unsettling sights evoked disgust, fear, and other Yin emotions within him.

Here we can see a variety of strange situations Naropa encountered, and also see that intense emotional reactions were the normal response. These were reactions that would raise anyone's Yin Qi or Yang Qi, which is the whole point of the story that may simply be a fabricated teaching lesson. Remember that you cannot just cultivate positive inner Yang energy but must purify your Yin energy as well, which is why so many of these events were steeped with Yin connotations.

The necessity to cultivate your Yin energies explains why some masters live in caves or in desolate, isolated places to absorb the Yin Prana of those locations (as well as to get away from hordes of devas). It also explains why many spiritual masters direct their students toward things they find repulsive, such as cemeteries, or frightening places. These experiences stimulate Yin Prana, something people rarely seek on their own.

When a purification session is conducted on you, any local devas in the vicinity will also want work done on their own subtle bodies. They may enter you during teaching sessions if an enlightened master is working on your purification. The process can be made so painful at times not just to raise your Yin Qi but to dissuade many devas from wanting to join in. You are being helped, but also being used like the end of a whip that is gradually frayed as Causal-bodied, Supra-Causal, and Immanence individuals demonstrate their skills using your body and mind – showing how delicately or strongly they can control their Prana by giving you and the attending devas varying painful sensations through multiple *nirmanakaya* emanations. This is symbolized in Tantric Hinduism and Vajrayana Buddhism by images of deities shown standing with their feet crushing human bodies, representing this relationship.

THE 10 TRIALS OF LU DONGBIN

Chinese Taoism offers its own story to illustrate the very same principles found in: (1) the churning of the Ocean of Milk story, which Taoism calls internal alchemy Qi rotations through the microcosmic and macrocosmic circulations of the human body, (2) the *Surangama Sutra* teachings on emotional states you will be put through during the lengthy kundalini purification process, (3) the thermal mapping studies revealing how intense emotions evoke body sensations connected to our internal energy, and (4) the story of Naropa's twelve minor hardships.

This story is a Chinese narrative about the ten trials of Lu Dongbin that mirrors Naropa's tale and the information provided by the *Surangama Sutra*. Lu Dongbin was a renowned Taoist who achieved enlightenment, namely the higher spiritual bodies of liberation, so the tale – fictional or not – represents what someone goes through before they can achieve the subtle body attainment.

Like Naropa's hardships and the ten trials described in the *Surangama Sutra*, Lu Dongbin's experiences teach us what to expect during the internal alchemy transformational process that washes your Prana so that your astral deva body can become differentiated from the rest of your Prana and break free of its physical shell. There will be provocations to evoke intense emotions that differentiate the Yin and Yang energies from each other in your body, allowing for a brief period of intense purification by higher beings.

The twelve minor trials of Naropa teach this exact same lesson. Similarly, Shakyamuni Buddha explicitly warned in the *Surangama Sutra* about this necessary process of stimulating intense emotions, cautioning practitioners not to let devas lead them astray into actions that violate common sense or laws during this time, otherwise you will get into trouble.

The Ten Trials of Lu Dongbin, though their deeper meaning remains largely unknown to Taoists, actually describe the Prana purification phase of the twelve-year kundalini transformation. During this period, Lu Dongbin experienced various powerful emotional states that stimulated his Prana so that it was clearly differentiated from the rest of his body's energy, and therefore could be more readily purified.

In the **First Trial**, Lu Dongbin experienced profound sadness (Yin energy activation) when he believed his family members were dying.

In the **Second Trial**, he felt intense anger (Yang energy activation) after being cheated in the marketplace while selling his goods.

In the **Third Trial**, he responded with compassion (activating Yang energy) to give money to a beggar, and then indignation and irritation (arousing Yin energy) because the beggar kept asking for more and more.

In the **Fourth Trial**, encountering a hungry tiger, Lu Dongbin was struck with overwhelming fear (stimulating his Yin Prana).

In the **Fifth Trial**, he successfully resisted powerful sexual desire (Yang energy activation) when a beautiful woman attempted to seduce him.

In the **Sixth Trial**, Lu Dongbin felt dejected and depressed (Yin energy activation) upon discovering his entire estate had been completely burglarized.

In the **Seventh Trial**, he experienced both astonishment and joy (Yang Prana activation) alongside the temptation of greed (Yin energy stimulation) when discovering that bronze utensils he purchased were actually gold – which he promptly returned.

In the **Eighth Trial**, Lu Dongbin summoned fearless courage (Yang energy activation) despite natural nervousness (Yin energy stimulation) when drinking a mysterious potion said to either grant enlightenment or cause death.

In the **Ninth Trial**, during a flood, he initially felt great worry and terror (Yin energy activation) before regaining his composure.

The **Tenth Trial** is the most revealing. It occurred as Lu Dongbin was reading alone in his room when countless ghosts, demons, and monsters seemingly emerged from everywhere to attack him (intensely activating his Yin Prana due to fright). Similar illusions of demonic attacks were reported by Christian saint Padre Pio and Tibetan adept Yeshe Tsogyel (c. 757), which were basically devas masquerading as devils and having a great time at it.

Despite the attacks, Lu Dongbin continued his chores while completely ignoring the demonic apparitions. One monster shouted that Lu Dongbin had wronged him in a previous life and must now sacrifice himself as payment. Without a trace of fear, Lu replied, "Take my life freely, since I took yours in a past life. This is only fair."

At that moment, the sound of clapping hands filled the air, followed by a triumphant shout. The sky suddenly cleared to brilliant blue, and all the ghosts and devils vanished. There stood his master, **Han Zhongli** (late Han dynasty 2nd-3rd century or Tang dynasty early 8th century), who had been observing and laughing throughout the entire ordeal.

In other words, Han Zhongli (along with other enlightened spiritual masters who were helping him) had orchestrated this elaborate illusion, creating both the apparitions and emotional provocations while simultaneously working to purify Lu Dongbin's inner subtle body energies. All the devas that he heard were inside his head while what he saw were just illusions perpetrated by his spiritual master, or someone higher helping out.

SUMMARY

This tale perfectly illustrates what happens during advanced internal alchemy – the twelve or more years (often twenty for beginners) required to purify your body's Prana. This purification allows your subtle body to differentiate itself from your body's impure energy. As the interface between physical and subtle bodies weakens due to the substances becoming more different than one another, your spirit body can finally break free. Throughout this process, masters deliberately provoke strong

Yin and Yang emotions to purify your Prana, most commonly masquerading as devils or demons to stimulate Yin energy through fear.

India's Aghori tradition and Tibet's Chöd practice specialize in this approach, deliberately placing practitioners in unpleasant circumstances to affect Yin Prana. Similarly, Jain monks cultivate extreme concern (anxiety) about harming even tiny insects, while Orthodox Christians practice deep humility and recite prayers lamenting their sinful nature and fear of Hell – all methods designed to raise Yin Prana.

Speaking frankly, the final stages of kundalini transformation can be extremely painful and challenging. Throughout this extended process, overseen by spiritual masters purifying your Prana through *nirmanakaya* emanations, numerous devas and lower spiritual beings move in and out of your brain and practice affecting your consciousness by giving you thoughts and emotions. They surround you daily, all seeking purification of their own subtle bodies to advance from an impure subtle body to a purified one – or even to achieve the Causal body.

During this lengthy purification process, you become a nexus of spiritual activity yet ordinary people have no clue as to what is happening to you. Group after group of heavenly beings passes through you daily, each attended by their own spiritual masters who work simultaneously on purifying your body and those of their students. As you receive transformation assistance, the local devas and other transiting students receive help too – this mutual benefit explaining why higher beings bother to invest more than a decade working on your transformation. Your enlightenment process facilitates hundreds to thousands of devas advancing to higher bodies simultaneously.

Established enlightened beings also seek purification efforts for their own *nirmanakaya* emanations, which would allow these projections to achieve their own higher body attainments so that their "owner" could do even more good deeds through them. When ancient masters work on you, they simultaneously assist many devas in your vicinity using hundreds of emanations to wash their Prana too, while teaching advanced skills to local guardian spirits on how to perform certain energy manipulations. You never undergo this process alone – all the "voices" you hear belong to devas whose Prana bodies are being purified alongside you. These entities typically enjoy playing tricks on humans and rarely provide useful information, making conversations with them largely meaningless. All masters will tell you to just ignore them.

On the spiritual path, devas and masters often masquerade as benevolent figures (angels, saints, deities, gods) to stimulate Yang Prana or malevolent ones (devils, demons) to stimulate your Yin Prana. Unfortunately, this sometimes reaches dangerous extremes as they become carried away with their ability to manipulate human consciousness. This is why Shakyamuni Buddha provided teachings to warn people against going astray, as I am doing now.

All the local devas desire enlightened masters to transform their Prana through *nirmanakaya* emanations – the most efficient path to ascension besides endless personal effort. To discourage unqualified aspirants from joining these training sessions within you, masters sometimes make the process exceptionally painful, causing many to leave (often placing thoughts of departure in the minds of unqualified attendees just as the thought to read the forbidden book was put in St. Poryphrios's mind). When others witness your suffering, no one complains, "Why him/her and not me?" The visible pain eliminates jealousy.

These secrets, though hidden from mainstream religion, appear in many spiritual traditions as the esoteric teachings. May this information benefit future generations of practitioners undergoing this challenging process.

Shakyamuni Buddha told his student Ananda, "After my *nirvana*, in the Dharma ending age, you must transmit this teaching so that all living beings may awaken to this message, that Deva *Mara* (heavenly demons) cannot take advantage of such states (to have their own way), and that practitioners can be on their guard as they strive to realize supreme enlightenment."

CHAPTER 6:
THE NON-SECTARIAN LADDER OF SPIRITUAL PROGRESS

Throughout this book, we have journeyed across time, geography, and diverse spiritual traditions to explore two extraordinary phenomena that have manifested with remarkable consistency in the lives of spiritual adepts: incorruptibility and bilocation. For many saints, bilocation was also accompanied by the performance of other miracles.

From the mountain monasteries of Tibet to the chapels of Mediterranean Europe, from the temples of India to the shrines of Japan, these manifestations transcend the boundaries of any single faith. These are non-sectarian phenomena which point to shared spiritual principles. What we have discovered is not a collection of isolated miracles but rather evidence of a universal spiritual process with consistent mechanics, prerequisites, and outcomes.

THE NON-SECTARIAN NATURE AND STEPS OF SPIRITUAL ASCENSION

Perhaps the most striking revelation of our exploration is the fundamentally non-denominational nature of bilocation and incorruptibility. These phenomena appear across Christianity, Hinduism, Buddhism, Islam, Judaism, Sikhism, Taoism, and other traditions with remarkable consistency in their essential features:

INCORRUPTIBLE BODIES AND BILOCATION MIRACLES

- Catholic saints like Padre Pio, who appeared simultaneously in San Giovanni Rotondo and distant battlefields, mirror the abilities of Hindu yogis like Neem Karoli Baba, who was seen simultaneously in Kainchi and at remote train stations.
- The incorruptible body of St. Bernadette Soubirous, found intact decades after her death, parallels the preservation of Buddhist monks like Luang Phu Waen Sujinno in Thailand or Dambo Lama Dashi-Dorzho Itigilov in Russia.
- The multiple manifestations of Taoist immortal Lu Dongbin appear conceptually identical to the spiritual emanations of Swaminarayan, Tibetan adepts or the simultaneous appearances of Islamic saints like Abdul Qadir Gilani.

In every tradition, these abilities emerge after years of intensive spiritual practice, often following periods of intense purification that include similar physical and psychological symptoms and sometimes common spiritual practices. While the outward forms of practice differ – Christian contemplative prayer, Buddhist meditation, Jewish prayer and study, Islamic *dhikr* (remembrance of Allah), Hindu mantra recitation and devotion, or Taoist internal alchemy – the underlying transformation of consciousness, the body and its energy follows remarkably similar patterns.

It is not that any religion or religious group is chosen or special. Anyone can achieve the progress that takes you up the spiritual ladder. You must simply set out on a path that purifies your mind, conduct and internal energy. If you don't do this then you are not following a religious path of ascension. Virtue and merit are the prerequisites of success, not your religious tradition. This is why individuals of every religion succeed.

This consistency points to a profound truth: the human potential for spiritual transcendence operates according to universal principles that transcend doctrinal boundaries. These phenomena are not the exclusive domain of any single faith but rather represent innate human capacities awakened through dedicated spiritual cultivation. The tradition you start with does not matter as long as you remain devoted to the practice of virtuous conduct, self-reflection and self-correction, inner silence, and various ways to move your internal energy.

THE FIVE BODIES: A FRAMEWORK FOR UNDERSTANDING TRANSCENDENCE

Eastern traditions, particularly Hinduism, Buddhism, Yoga, Tantra and Taoism, offer a comprehensive framework for understanding these extraordinary abilities through the concept of the "five bodies." This framework of five bodies, which finds parallels in the esoteric teachings of nearly all major faiths, explains both bilocation and incorruptibility as natural expressions of spiritual development:

1. **Physical Body** (*annamaya kosha* or form *skandha*): Our material form composed of gross matter. This is the level of the human being.
2. **Subtle Body** (*pranamaya kosha* or sensation *skandha*): The energy body composed of Prana or Qi (life force), which can separate from the physical body through intensive spiritual practice. This is the attainment level of an asura or deva who both have subtle energy bodies. They are capable of either the first or second dhyana (*vitarka* or *vicara samadhi*) that corresponds to the Srotapanna and Sakadagamin stages of Arhatship.
3. **Causal Body** (*manomaya kosha* or conception *skandha*): A higher spiritual body that emerges through continued purification of the subtle body. This is the level of an Anagamin Arhat who can access the third dhyana, or *ananda samadhi* of Hinduism.
4. **Supra-Causal Body** (*vijnanamaya kosha* or volition *skandha*): A transcendental form that exists beyond space-time limitations, capable of manifesting *nirmanakaya* (emanation bodies) simultaneously in multiple locations. This is the stage of a full Arhat who has achieved *nirvana* with remainder, and who is capable of the *asmita samadhi*.
5. **Superconsciousness Body** (*anandamaya kosha* or consciousness *skandha*): The highest spiritual attainment of the Immanence, Superconsciousness or Tathagata body represents complete unity with universal life. This is the stage of a Great Golden Arhat who has achieved *nirvana* without remainder because he has attained Perfect and Complete Enlightenment, a stage of no more learning.

This progressive emergence of higher spiritual bodies explains how an individual might appear in multiple places simultaneously. The phenomenon we call "bilocation" actually represents the ability of those who have attained the Supra-Causal or Superconsciousness body that can project tangible *nirmanakaya* emanations that can be seen, heard, and even touched by others, or what people actually see might be the actual Supra-Causal or Superconsciousness body of the saint/sage himself that has materialized into a tangible body of form.

When a saint achieves these higher bodies they become the new center of their life, and the human body we see is just a living shell they leave behind to use like an appendage.

It is not the human body that generates these higher bodies and their manifestations. The higher bodies are the new center of life for the individual, and they generate the *nirmanakaya* emanations or perform tangible materializations themselves. Movies always depict this incorrectly by showing that a human being generates a spiritual body. The actual case is that you cultivate for years to finally free the energies of a higher body from within the matrix of your present energies, that transcendental body becomes the new center of your life, and it is only the successors to your released subtle body (Arhat stage or higher) that are capable of generating *nirmanakaya* projections. A human body cannot do it no matter what type of magic shown by movies or comic books.

The human body that was the original template is never involved with such things at all and doesn't even know that they are occurring because they are caused by the real man who is now independent of his lower natures. The human body is not his self and is incapable of miraculous feats. They are all performed by the higher human who has attained higher bodies.

The bilocation bodies are not mere apparitions but actual spiritual bodies that can condense their energy into matter, or they are *nirmanakaya* that are functional extensions of consciousness made of very refined energies that can perform special actions.

Similarly, incorruptibility results from the profound purification of the physical body during the lengthy process of spiritual transformation one must go through that is necessary for attaining these higher purified bodies. The continuous circulation and refinement of Prana/Qi throughout the body for years (typically a minimum of twelve) purifies the body tissues so profoundly that even after death, the body resists normal decomposition processes.

THE ALCHEMY OF PRANA PURIFICATION

At the heart of bilocation and incorruptibility lies the purification of Prana or Qi, the vital energy that animates our body and spirit. This process happens to all spiritual saints regardless of their tradition and is best explained through the lens of kundalini transformation, a 12- to 20-year ordeal of internal alchemy that differentiates one's pure Prana from impure Prana, a process akin to churning butter from milk. This process, universal across traditions but symbolized in the Hindu *Samudra Manthana* (Churning of the Ocean of Milk), involves purifying your own internal energies together through intense emotional and energetic experiences orchestrated by enlightened beings.

The mechanics of this purification process appear consistently across traditions:

1. **Differentiation of Energies**: Through intensive spiritual practice, the practitioner begins to differentiate the Yin and Yang aspects of their internal energy, a process symbolized in Hinduism by the "Churning of the Ocean of Milk" (*Samudra Manthana*).
2. **Emotional Catalysts**: As outlined in the Buddhist *Surangama Sutra*, the process always involves experiencing intense emotional states – from profound fear to boundless joy, from crushing sadness to liberating peace – that serve to stimulate different aspects of internal energy for purification. Thermal pictures of emotional-sensation responses highlight this connection between the mind/emotions and the body's vital energy.
3. **Testing Through Trials**: As illustrated by the Ten Trials of Lu Dongbin, the Twelve Minor Hardships of Naropa, and the ten types of Mara attacks described within the *Surangama Sutra*, the practitioner faces orchestrated spiritual challenges designed to evoke the powerful emotional states required to further the purification process.
4. **Physical Symptoms**: Practitioners universally report similar physical manifestations during this process: inner rolling energy sensations, intense heat (as with Padre Pio's medically inexplicable fevers of 118°F), bone-chilling cold (as experienced by Zen master Hakuin), physical trembling, spontaneous bodily movements, and unusual sensory phenomena. These are cataloged in Roman Catholicism, and also in the schools of Yoga, Taoism, Hinduism and Buddhism.

5. **Divine Assistance**: Across traditions, this transformation is understood to require the assistance of higher spiritual beings – whether conceived as devas, angels, Arhats, gurus, spiritual masters, or saints – who help direct and accelerate the purification through their own spiritual emanations or direct intercessions. Their assistance is an act of grace.

The *Surangama Sutra's* "Fifty Mara Deva States," Naropa's Twelve Minor Hardships, and Lu Dongbin's Ten Trials all illustrate how practitioners endure provoked emotions – fear, compassion, lust, pride – that stimulate their Yin and Yang Prana for purification. By provoking certain intense emotions one can accentuate related Prana flows, which then become highly differentiated from the rest of the body's energies, which are thus easier to purify.

Similarly, demonic assaults reveal a deliberate stirring of Yin energies based upon fear and anxiety, guided by masters using *nirmanakaya* emanations or their own body's energies. This churning, often painful and accompanied by physical symptoms like heat, cold, or illness, refines the internal subtle body, enabling incorruptibility after death. Bilocation is enabled as a standard ability when one attains the level of the Arhat or Great Golden Arhat body.

This process unfolds not in isolation but within a complex spiritual ecosystem. The practitioner undergoing transformation becomes a nexus for the simultaneous advancement of numerous spiritual beings, including local devas (subtle-bodied beings) who seek their own advancement to higher spiritual bodies. The soon-to-be saint will hear the group's laughter as their own bodies are purified along with his own during the long process as they will aggregate in his brain for teachings.

The process's universality – described as Christian mortification, Taoist internal alchemy, Hindu kundalini purification, Buddhist meditation, etcetera – underscores a singular path to transcendence beneath diverse terminologies.

A SHARED TRANSFORMATIVE PROCESS

The accounts we have seen reveal a strikingly similar process across traditions, marked by rigorous spiritual discipline, emotional trials, and divine assistance. Saints like Padre Pio, enduring demonic visions, and

Ramakrishna, appearing in Kolkata while physically in Dakshineswar, underwent decades of spiritual practice – prayer, meditation, fasting, study or asceticism – to purify their Prana.

The *Surangama Sutra* warns of "Mara" illusions – visions, sounds, or sensations – that test practitioners, a caution echoed in Ramana Maharshi's dismissal of miraculous displays. Physical phenomena, such as Padre Pio's heat and teachings given by Tamil Siddha saints, reflect the kundalini's "fire of separation" that slowly detaches the subtle body from its physical shell by purifying it so much that it no longer resembles its physical counterparts at its interfaces, which Buddhism calls *ching-se* or "clear matter."

Incorruptibility, seen in examples across spiritual traditions, results from this purification process that cleanses and thus preserves the body as a testament to spiritual attainment. The involvement of higher beings, whether spiritual masters or Arhats, ensures the process's success, as seen in the purification of local devas' bodies alongside human aspirants. This shared ordeal, demanding the cooperation of countless saints and spiritual masters working on one individual over the years, unites saints across traditions in the common task of helping that individual (and local devas) achieve spiritual liberation.

During this lengthy purification process, you become a nexus of spiritual activity, yet ordinary people have no clue as to what is happening to you. Group after group of heavenly beings passes through you daily, each attended by their own spiritual masters who work simultaneously on purifying your body and those of their students, whom you will often hear laughing in a happy group for joy is the main characteristic that describes devas. As you receive the transformation assistance of your Prana becoming purified, the local devas and transiting students receive help too – this mutual benefit explaining why higher beings are willing to invest more than a decade working on your transformation. Your enlightenment process facilitates hundreds of devas advancing to higher bodies simultaneously.

On the spiritual path, devas and masters often masquerade as benevolent figures (angels, saints, gods) to stimulate Yang Prana or malevolent ones (devils, demons) to stimulate Yin Prana through fear, anxiety or terror. This explains how many historical accounts of spiritual warfare with demons, particularly in Christian hagiography, can be understood through the lens of this purification process. What saints like Anthony the Great or Padre Pio experienced as demonic attacks were often orchestrated experiences designed to stimulate their Yin energy through fear and terror, thereby advancing their purification. The spiritual greats of every tradition, including Moslems and Jews, also pass through these uncomfortable experiences but without his specific information they have no idea as to what is happening.

GUIDANCE FOR CONTEMPORARY SEEKERS

For those on the spiritual path today, the phenomena explored in this book offer both inspiration and caution:

1. **The Universality of the Path**: Seekers should recognize that authentic spiritual transformation transcends religious boundaries. The path of spiritual ascendancy – also called glorification, deification, divinization, liberation or enlightenment – is non-denominational. Therefore, while honoring one's chosen tradition, one might benefit from understanding the universal principles that underlie the diverse spiritual practices for cultivating the ladder of ascension.
2. **The Necessity of Guidance**: The kundalini purification process described herein is intense and potentially dangerous without proper guidance and protection. Across traditions, those who successfully navigate this transformation typically do so in safe locations, and usually under the tutelage, guidance and protection of realized masters who understand its mechanics.
3. **Virtue as Foundation**: Consistently across traditions, bilocation and incorruptibility emerge not through techniques alone but because the individual cultivated profound virtue, ethical conduct, non-violence and compassion that are foundational requirements that qualify one for the path of ascension. The generation of higher spiritual bodies appears contingent upon virtue and merit achieved through good deeds and ethical refinement, suggesting that moral cultivation remains essential to spiritual advancement.
4. **Beyond Phenomena**: While many of the miraculous abilities recorded may inspire awe, nearly all traditions caution against fixating on supernatural phenomena. They are just normal abilities for all the human beings living in each higher spiritual realm. Saints who demonstrated bilocation typically downplayed these abilities, focusing instead on service and spiritual realization. As Ramana Maharshi

cautioned his students not to be distracted by visions or powers, the true goal remains inner transformation rather than hankering after superpowers that cannot come unless you attain the higher spiritual bodies in the first place.

A CALL TO SPIRITUAL PRACTICE

Bilocation and incorruptibility are not mere curiosities but beacons indicating the heights of human potential, and illuminate the transformative power of spiritual cultivation practices. They reveal that sanctity is not confined to one faith but is a universal heritage, accessible through the alchemy of Prana purification that leads to spiritual ascension. The shared process – marked by emotional trials, energetic rotations of energy inside oneself, and divine collaboration – offers a roadmap for aspirants, tempered by sobering insights into its uncomfortable challenges.

As we conclude our exploration of bilocation and incorruptibility across spiritual traditions, we are left with a profound vision of human potential. Beyond the dogmatic divisions that have so often separated religious communities, these phenomena reveal *a shared blueprint for spiritual transformation that transcends cultural and historical boundaries.*

The evidence suggests that the capacity for spiritual transcendence – including the generation of multiple spiritual bodies capable of simultaneous manifestation and the transformation of physical matter beyond normal biological constraints – represents *an innate human potential.* Though relatively rare, these abilities have emerged consistently across civilizations and epochs whenever individuals have undertaken the rigorous process of spiritual purification through an ardent path of religious practices.

That's the key – if you devote yourself to religious practices then you can achieve these transformations, but it is a shame that in today's world the public is turning away from Church attendance, meditation, prayer and the other very methods that transform/purify their internal energies. Once they pass away, people typically regret the fact that "no one told them," they wasted all that time, and now they furiously pursue all sorts of methods to cultivate their purity, running from one enlightened master to the next hoping to get some purification work done on their body.

Perhaps most significantly, these phenomena point toward a unifying principle behind diverse religious expressions. While the outer forms of spiritual practice differ – Christian prayer, Buddhist meditation, Hindu yoga, Taoist internal alchemy, Jewish self-reflection, Moslem *dikhr* and remembrance – the inner transformation follows remarkably consistent patterns. This suggests that beneath the surface diversity of the world's spiritual traditions lies a common core of experiential truth accessible through dedicated practice, such as revealed within *Arhat Yoga* and *Buddha Yoga* (which cover all religions), *Correcting Zen* (which covers Buddhism), *The Secret Inner Teachings of Daoism* (which covers Daoism), *Hidden Teachings in Hinduism* (which covers Hinduism), *Neijia Yoga* (which covers marital arts and Vajrayana), *Nyasa Yoga* (which covers Tantra) or *Color Me Confucius* (which covers Confucianism). This book clearly reveals that Christianity, Judaism, and Islam have many of the same liberation teachings as in the East, and shows that the western saints achieve the same stages of spiritual ascendance. Jews, Christians and Moslems who cultivate sufficiently can all achieve the same heavenly stages of liberation.

As science and spirituality continue to evolve in dialogue, perhaps these remarkable cases will someday bridge the apparent gap between material and spiritual understanding, as well as the gap between eastern and western religions. By examining these phenomena through both ancient wisdom and modern scientific frameworks, we may develop a more comprehensive understanding of the potential spiritual stages of human existence and their relationship to physical reality – one that honors both the universal principles underlying spiritual transformation and the diverse cultural expressions through which that transformation has been pursued across history.

Let the lives of these saints – Padre Pio, Rabbi Isaac Luria, Swaminarayan, Lu Dongbin, Hui Neng and countless others – serve as a call to purify body, mind, and spirit, forging a legacy of sanctity that endures beyond the grave. In this unified vision, the boundaries between traditions fade not into homogeneity but into a recognition of complementary perspectives on the same fundamental truths. The saint, the yogi, the Sheikh, the *tzadik*, the Buddhist master, the guru, the prophet, spiritual master and the Taoist immortal each offer a distinct yet convergent path toward the same reality: a transcendence of ordinary limitations through a spiritual path of practice that earns one nearly immortal transcendental spiritual bodies.

FURTHER RREADING

To go beyond this book you are encouraged to read the following in order: *Hidden Teachings in Hinduism* (Bodri), *The Secret Inner Teachings of Daoism* (Bodri), *Anthonite Fathers and Anthonite Matters* (Paisios), *Traditional Theory of Evolution and Its Application in Yoga* (Gharote, Devnath, and Jha), *Correcting Zen* (Bodri), and *Arhat Yoga* (Bodri).

Arhat Yoga is the foundational text that explains the commonalities of the spiritual path for all religions, but because it's a thick book you should start with these other reading materials. Once you understand *Hidden Teachings in Hinduism* and *The Secret Inner Teachings of Daoism* you'll be better able to comprehend the universal template within *Arhat Yoga*.

Next, for deep instructions on the how-to-do instructions for spiritual practice please read *Nyasa Yoga* (Bodri) and *Neijia Yoga* (Bodri). These books teach the basics of *neijia* or *nei-gong* work in abbreviated form, especially *Neijia Yoga*. For an understanding of the wide variety of *neijia* methods available across world religions, you should reference *Hidden Teachings in Hinduism* and *The Secret Inner Teachings of Daoism* for the list of methods that employ emotions to excite your Qi-Prana, or spiritual cultivation techniques that guide your internal Qi-Prana using your thoughts (willpower), sounds, physical movements or other methods.

Another useful practice book for some people might be *A Systematic Course in the Ancient Tantric Techniques of Yoga and Kriya* (Swami Saraswati) and the yoga books of B.K.S. Iyengar. Locally you can always find someone to teach yoga as well as soft martial arts such as *taijiquan*, *xingyiquan* and *baguazhuang* that stress internal energy exercises in their tradition.

Color Me Confucius (Bodri) and *Buddha Yoga* (Bodri) will guide you through basic spiritual information as well as methods for cultivating your personality, conduct and determining your life purpose.

To better understand the stages of the spiritual path you can read *Meditation Case Studies* (Bodri) and *The Little Book of Hercules* (Bodri).

Overall these books will give a fuller picture of the spiritual path and its transformation processes on your mind and body. You will also learn more details on the kundalini process of spiritual transformation, which Taoism calls inner alchemy or transmutation, and which Christianity calls divinization, deification or glorification.

www.ingramcontent.com/pod-product-compliance
Lightning Source LLC
Chambersburg PA
CBHW072015070526
44583CB00015B/1492